Foreigners In Spain
Triumphs & Disasters

edited by
Graeme Chesters

SURVIVAL BOOKS • LONDON • ENGLAND

First published 2004

Survival Books Limited, 1st Floor,
60 St James's Street, London SW1A 1ZN, United Kingdom
☎ +44 (0)20-7493 4244, ▤ +44 (0)20-7491 0605
✉ info@survivalbooks.net
▣ www.survivalbooks.net
To order books, please refer to page 220.

British Library Cataloguing in Publication Data.
A CIP record for this book is available
from the British Library.
ISBN 1 901130 43 6

Printed and bound in Finland by WS Bookwell Ltd

ACKNOWLEDGEMENTS

M y thanks go to everybody who replied to our questionnaire and submitted themselves to further probing, via email, on the telephone or in person. To those individuals whose tales we didn't put in the book, please don't take it personally; it was usually because they were similar to ones included. Thanks to my wife Louise for helping me to choose which stories to include and for an initial proofreading. As ever, special thanks to Joe and Kerry Laredo for editing, final proofreading and desktop publishing, and to Jim Watson for the superb cartoons, which (irritatingly) encapsulate as much information as that contained in many paragraphs of carefully constructed prose.

TITLES BY SURVIVAL BOOKS

The Alien's Guide To Britain;
The Alien's Guide To France;
The Best Places To Live
In France; The Best Places To
Live In Spain; Buying, Selling &
Letting Property;
Foreigners In France: Triumphs
& Disasters; Foreigners In Spain:
Triumphs & Disasters;
How To Avoid Holiday &
Travel Disasters;
Costa del Sol Lifeline;
Dordogne/Lot Lifeline;
Poitou-Charentes Lifeline;
Renovating & Maintaining Your
French Home; Retiring Abroad;
Rioja And Its Wines;
The Wines Of Spain

Living And Working Series

Abroad; America; Australia;
Britain; Canada; The European
Union; The Far East; France;
Germany; The Gulf States &
Saudi Arabia; Holland, Belgium
& Luxembourg; Ireland; Italy;
London; New Zealand; Spain;
Switzerland

Buying A Home Series

Abroad; Florida;
France; Greece & Cyprus;
Ireland; Italy;
Portugal; Spain

Order forms are on page 220.

ABOUT THE EDITOR

Graeme Chesters was born in the north-west of England in 1963, obtained a degree in philosophy at Bristol University and worked in the City of London for ten years. He has lived in Spain since 1995. He's a columnist for a Spanish newspaper, contributes to British newspapers and magazines, and writes wine, travel and children's books. He's the author of *How to Avoid Holiday and Travel Disasters, Living and Working in The Gulf States & Saudi Arabia* and *The Wines of Spain,* all published by Survival Books.

Lo que en los libros no está, la vida te enseñará.

Spanish proverb

'There is much to be learned from books,
but life is the best teacher.'

CONTENTS

STORIES

Second-Class Citizenship 11

Short & Mostly Sweet 23

Cutting And Running 29

Deliverance 39

English As A Foreign Language 51

Season Ticket 61

Costa Del Concrete 71

Life In A Warm Climate 81

Close Encounters 91

Mixed Feelings 103

Living It Down In Madrid 121

A Good Choice 133

Best Of Both Worlds 143

A Perfect Retirement 153

Different From Denmark 163

A Volcanic Career   171

Happy Penury   181

Cut Off On The Costa Blanca   189

Unchained Melody   199

Highway To Happiness   209

ORDER FORMS   220

EDITOR'S NOTES

- British English is used except in stories told by North Americans, where American English vocabulary and spelling have been retained.
- Spanish words are italicised and an English translation has been given in brackets where appropriate.
- The following symbols are used in this book: ☎ (telephone), 📄 (fax), 💻 (internet) and ✉ (email).

Important Note

From the many stories offered to us, I've chosen those that I thought would be the most interesting and instructive to readers and have attempted to include as wide as possible a variety of nationalities, situations and geographical locations. I haven't selected contributors on the basis of any prejudice or bias as to nationality, opinions or any other criteria.

All the stories have been written by the people they relate to and none has been changed in any factual detail; only minor changes have been made in the interest of clarity and readability. No attempt has been made to paint a rosy (or any other kind of) picture of Spain; there are positive and negative opinions, which aren't necessarily those of the editor or the publisher. Some contributors have asked to be referred to by pseudonyms – a request which I have respected.

Any information and advice offered by contributors has been provided in good faith, but it shouldn't be used as the basis of any major decisions or irrevocable action. For authoritative and unbiased information, you're recommended to obtain the latest edition of a book such as Survival Books' *The Best Places to Buy a Home in Spain, Buying a Home in Spain* or *Living and Working in Spain* (see page 220). **Nevertheless, you shouldn't believe everything you read, and all information should be checked with an independent and reliable source.**

INTRODUCTION

Moving to a foreign country can be traumatic; it can also be an exciting and life-enhancing experience. The people who have told their stories in this book have had successes as well as failures and are well qualified to offer advice to others contemplating life as an expatriate.

As several of them have said, living in Spain isn't always the idyllic dream that's conjured up in television programmes and in travelogue books. Spain – and the Spanish – can be challenging, difficult and even downright insufferable. As one of my contributors says, "People often think it's all sweetness and light. It isn't – but then nowhere is." Nevertheless, the majority of contributors are glad they moved to Spain and, given a second chance, would do so again.

If you're thinking of going to live in Spain, you will need to obtain the latest edition of an authoritative book (or two) such as Survival Books' *Living and Working in Spain, Buying a Home in Spain* and *The Best Places to Buy a Home in Spain* (see page 220) for the essential information that will help you avoid pitfalls and prevent your dream turning into a nightmare.

Foreigners in Spain: Triumphs & Disasters is a vital companion to those volumes, providing personal and emotional accounts of life in Spain, which will instruct, amuse, surprise, shock and – hopefully – inspire you.

Of course, people's experiences are unique, and generalisations aren't always valid. If you move to Spain, you will no doubt have different experiences, but these stories may help you to anticipate and overcome the problems and obstacles that you encounter. 'A problem shared is a problem halved' goes the saying; when you realise that yours have been encountered by others, you will find them much easier to cope with.

There's no magic formula for a successful life in Spain, but another of my contributors sensibly recommends the following ingredients: "one healthy sense of adventure, a dash of caution, a large dollop of preparation, and a good measure of hard work. Stir well and you might just have created the recipe for a happy expatriate life."

¡Mucha suerte!

Graeme Chesters
July 2004

Second-Class Citizenship

Susan Hughes from Merseyside swapped a
high-flying career in fashion for motherhood on Mijas
Costa. Having children was relatively straightforward;
making Spanish friends was not.

We didn't come to Spain because we were unhappy in Britain but to open our own restaurant. My husband had always been interested in food and wanted to go into the business. He did some restaurant training in London and Brussels, and also took a course in Italy. The original idea was to open in either London or Brussels – London because that is where we lived, Brussels because that is where Steve's family was based for half the year. But after a bit of research, we realised that both of them would have been expensive and risky, so Steve's parents suggested Spain, where they lived for the other half of the year.

They had bought some land and built a villa on Mijas Costa about fifteen years previously, so we knew the area, having been out many times on holiday. And it looked as if it would be cheaper to open a restaurant in Spain, so we took the plunge. As well as wanting to open our own business, I was becoming bored with my job in London and I think my biological alarm clock was starting to go off, and we thought that Spain would be a nice environment in which to bring up children.

When we told people what we were planning to do, I think quite a lot of them thought we wouldn't actually go through with it. But I don't think my family were particularly surprised, because I had already moved from home to Nottingham, Leicester and London, and this was just another move, but with sea between us now rather than motorway.

A Long Hard Shock

When we finally arrived in Spain, it was a great big culture shock. Looking back, I think I was a bit naïve and over-optimistic to expect it to be an easy transition and not to be as different as it actually was, and so I was unprepared. The worst aspect of it was that I found it very difficult for a woman to be taken seriously. Whenever we were dealing with anything to do with setting up the business or taking deliveries, people would always want to deal with Steve. It isn't as bad for women now as it was when we arrived, but the attitude still persists to some extent. I suppose that it has got better because there are many more foreigners here now and the locals are better used to dealing with foreign women.

I was also dismayed by the *mañana* attitude in Spain. I knew it existed, of course, but not that it was so deep-rooted, and I quickly began to wonder how anybody ever got anything done. It was a big surprise to find how unprofessional and even slapdash everything seemed to be. In order to open a restaurant in Spain you need all sorts of licences and permits, and we waited weeks longer than we had expected before we could open.

So I didn't have the easiest start to life in Spain, but it was probably made worse by my hormones, because I fell pregnant only a couple of months after we arrived here. It was unplanned because we had intended to set up the business first and establish it before trying for a baby. But after arriving in September, I was pregnant by November, which probably added to my sense of being unsettled.

> *it takes a lot longer to get a restaurant business up, running and known than you might expect*

The language was another barrier. We had had a few Spanish lessons in England and learned the basics, but we naïvely assumed that it would be easy to build on that and pick up the language once we were living here. It wasn't. I wish we had done more before we arrived, because once you are here and have a business that attracts mainly British customers, as we had, you get little chance to practise. And it is all too easy to do nothing about improving your Spanish, unless you are forced to, which we weren't.

I think it took me a couple of years to settle in and relax in Spain. It took me that long to get over wondering why we had done it. I also think that moving into our own house here helped. Before that, when we were living in a flat above the restaurant, it felt temporary, rather than that we were building a home.

But looking back on the move to Spain, it might have been rather less of a shock to have moved to Madrid or Barcelona rather than to Fuengirola. Because we didn't just move from one country to another, but we went from London, one of the biggest – most sophisticated and cosmopolitan cities in the world – to Fuengirola, which is basically a large fishing village, with attitudes to match.

Another thing that I experienced when I came to Spain was a sense that I no longer had much status or worth. Back in England, after a degree at Trent Polytechnic, I had worked as a ladies' fashion buyer at various firms, including River Island, Principles and Next. It was a responsible job and I had had a team working under me, a company car and business-class trips abroad to places like the South of France and India. But when I came to Spain, all that was gone and it took me quite a long time to shake off the sense that I wasn't as worthwhile any more. Maybe it would have happened if we had stayed in the UK and I had given up work and had children, but perhaps it was made worse by coming here and, as a woman, being treated as a second-class citizen. And being pregnant and then having a newborn to look after, I couldn't pull my weight in the business as we had intended and that probably added to my sense of purposelessness.

Getting Up & Running

Our experience in Spain has been that it takes a lot longer to get a restaurant business up, running and known than you might expect. As well as the delays with paperwork that I mentioned earlier, you find that suppliers often deliver late, which can cause major hassles. And some suppliers are reluctant to deal with new businesses, which is understandable when you consider how many new operations fold, owing money to all and sundry. We also found that, if you have any alterations or building work done, it is wise to get a few quotes, because prices vary widely, with both Spanish and British workmen.

And we found that it takes quite a long time to attract enough custom to turn a profit, however good you are and however well located. Without being too arrogant about it – which of course means that I am about to be just that! – we were good and located in a lovely setting. But you are competing with the fact that there are too many restaurants in this part of the world and people can eat lunch and dinner at a different place every day of the year.

It takes some time to appear on people's radar, longer to attract them back a second time and ages for them to become regulars. I think that is something which people underestimate when they come to run a bar or restaurant in Spain. With it being a popular tourist destination, they seem to assume that there will be an endless stream of custom, but it isn't that easy. You have to put in the time and work in order to build a name and reputation, and let it spread.

they aren't very generous with the pain killers that expectant mothers take for granted in Britain

So if you are planning a bar or restaurant here, think long and hard about it first. What exactly are you going to offer and how will you stand out from the rest? We came to Spain having planned our business quite well and with Steve having trained first, which is more than quite a lot of people do – they come with no planning or prior experience and wonder why they fail. Even with planning and prior experience, most people struggle at first.

Another thing about the restaurant business is the anti-social hours it involves. Steve worked six nights per week, as well as having to buy and prepare food during the day. By the time our two children had arrived, the restaurant had become busy for quite a lot of the year, so Steve hardly had time to see the kids. That is really the reason we decided to open a cafeteria and delicatessen, so he could work days rather than nights, which are much more normal and social hours and what we had become used to in England. He sees a bit more of the kids at convenient times of the day and it is also better for his sanity and stress levels.

I also get to see more of him, although I am quite independent and like my own company so I didn't sit at home sulking when he worked nights. But I do remember sitting watching the American comedy 'Friends' one night on my own and smiling to myself as I thought that these people were my only friends at the moment.

Baby Comes First

I have been very impressed with the health system in Spain. The doctors adopt a no-nonsense approach, which I like, and they don't faff about or mollycoddle you, but just get on with the treatment. Their approach during my pregnancies was very professional but the mother is seen very much as the host, the baby being the more important part of the equation. They are also concerned about how you are, but mainly as to how your health affects the baby. If you complain of an aching back, for example, they are unimpressed and will say, "Of course you have a sore back, you're pregnant," and expect you to get on with it.

Even at the hospital for the birth, they are still focused very much on the baby, not the mother. So they aren't very generous with the pain killers that expectant mothers in Britain take for granted, and you have to be half dying in order to get an epidural. The lack of care after the birth came as a bit of a shock. You have to travel to them to get it yourself if you want it; home aftercare is rarely given in Spain, because the family is expected to rally round to help, with grandmother giving the lessons in baby care rather than a nurse or midwife.

If you want to see a doctor the same day in Spain, you have to go to the emergency room and queue because your doctor probably won't be able to give you an appointment immediately; you're normally seen within a week. And there are always plenty of people waiting to see their doctor because the Spanish have a reputation for being hypochondriacs, who are at their happiest when they are taking a course of tablets – preferably several courses. Generally, however, I would say that the Spanish healthcare system is better than the British one, or better than I get the impression that the British one is – I haven't lived there for over eight years.

School Rules

We have been happy with the school our two boys attend, but it has a reputation as one of the better ones in the area, and standards do seem to vary quite a lot between schools. Teachers in Spain teach very much by the book and they will cover exactly what is in the set curriculum, to the letter, especially in secondary school. But it seems to work because I would say that our two – who are now aged six and eight – are at a slightly higher level overall than they would have been had they been educated in England. For example, the younger one, Leon, is already starting to learn times tables, although the teacher did say that this is early even by local standards.

It is a Spanish school and so, as might be expected, the one area in which they are behind where they would have been in England is English writing and reading. I think that they are about a year behind where they should be. But they have both been going to private English lessons since they were five, twice a week for two hours each time. So they will catch up in due course and they also start English lessons at 'normal' school when they are eight or nine, although I don't know how much use these will be to them by then. The great compensation of their being educated in Spanish and speaking English at home is that they are being brought up to be bilingual in two of the world's most spoken languages, which is a definite advantage.

There aren't many foreign pupils at Joe and Leon's school. When they started, they were the only ones in their classes, but there are a few more now. My two haven't had any problems specifically because they are foreign, but we did decide not to send the older boy, Joe, to one particular school because he is blond and very obviously not Spanish, and the school concerned had a lot of gypsy children who apparently caused a lot of problems. I am not being racist by saying that, just stating a fact. That school has apparently improved a lot recently because the gypsy kids don't go there any more. The area they lived in is being redeveloped to build a hypermarket so their families were moved somewhere else.

Most of the teachers at our boys' school don't speak English, although some of them understand it and there is one who is pretty good, who you can turn to in an emergency. But you usually need to speak reasonable Spanish in order to communicate with the teachers if your children go to a Spanish state school. But I do wonder at the attitude of some foreign parents to the question of language learning. When we were deciding which school to send our boys to, I went along with a friend to a meeting at a school in Calahonda, which is just up the coast, to the west of Fuengirola. The school concerned has a large percentage of foreign children and the teachers were beginning to worry about many of the foreign children's lack of knowledge of the Spanish language. So a meeting was called in order to discuss laying on extra Spanish lessons for the foreign children to get them up to speed. The lessons were to be voluntary and with a nominal charge, but the parents – most of them British – voted against the proposal because of the charge. I found that embarrassing, ignorant and short-sighted.

There are plenty of after-school activities available in Spain to which you can send your children and they are usually decently run and inexpensive. To go swimming three times a week for a month, for example, costs around €10 for members and €15 for non-members, while football and basketball are only €8 or €9 a month.

Something that might come as a shock to parents who have brought their children from other countries is that there is a three-month school summer holiday in Spain, beginning in late June, when the weather becomes really hot. Fortunately for us parents, summer schools have taken off in Spain over the last few years but, when my children were very young, it was difficult to be a working mother because the country wasn't really geared up for looking after the children. I suppose the attitude was the same as it is with looking after a new baby: grandmother will do it – so there were no other options.

My kids go to summer school here and in the state sector it is very cheap because it is subsidised. We pay less than €90 each for my two is for a month's summer school, from 9am to 2pm, five days a week. Private summer school is a lot more expensive – about €300 per child for a month, between 9am and 3.30pm, but it does include a three-course lunch.

All Life Is Here

The best things for us about living in Spain are the relaxed attitude to life and the emphasis on the family, including a tolerance of children that you don't see in Britain. People here tend to be calm and don't get over-excited about stupid things – you probably won't see a Spaniard indulging in road rage, for example. And it is great to be able to take children into bars and restaurants, where they aren't just allowed but actively welcomed. As a result of that, children become used to going out, they don't feel the need to show off and so they behave better, unlike some foreign children who play up in a new environment like a restaurant.

> *one of the worst things about living here is the rain, which I never minded in the UK. Southern Spain cannot cope with rain*

From what I see and read of the UK, I think that Spain is a better environment for children. It is gentler and safer, and the weather means that they can have an outdoor lifestyle, rather than sitting in front of a TV or computer screen, eating junk food and getting fat, which is what I read is happening in Britain. And children there seem to become adults before they are eleven, secondary schools are often poor and drugs are a problem. But children here have the chance to be children, at least for a while.

One of the worst things about living here is the rain, which I never minded in the UK. Southern Spain cannot cope with rain: everything floods and the electricity goes off. They really need to sort that out. I also don't like August, which is the main holiday month. It gets so hot and crowded, you can't drive anywhere, there is nowhere to park and you cannot get anything done. And our town gets inundated with Spaniards from Cordoba and other inland towns, and Moroccans, all coming to avoid the even greater summer heat where they live. Running the cafeteria in town means that we see a lot of these people and they are almost universally unpopular with shop, bar and restaurant owners in Fuengirola – Spanish and foreign alike – because they don't spend much. In fact, the Cordobeses have a reputation for bringing an entire month's groceries down with them for the length of their holiday. They take their own food and drink to the beach, but will occasionally descend en masse on a bar or ice cream parlour – mum, dad, kids, cousins, aunties, grandparents, the lot – where they order a handful of drinks costing next to nothing and sit for ages, taking up several tables and putting very little in the owner's pocket.

We find that this type of thing happens in the café, with big groups of inland Spaniards and Moroccans brooding over a couple of coffees for indecently long periods of time. They sometimes even have the cheek to buy cakes in the bakery opposite and try to eat them in our café. And we get queues of people who don't buy a thing but come to use our toilets. Running a café, bar or restaurant also means you are prey to weirdoes and nutters. For example, we had a man in here who sat at one of our tables and wet himself. He then carried on sitting there, oblivious, and seemed surprised when we asked him to leave. You do get to see all life, which is both good and bad.

Snobbery & Intolerance

Another slight downside to living on the Costa del Sol is that you have to be extra careful about not getting ripped off. It isn't because there are any more conmen here than there are anywhere else, but because of the language. For example, when we had the restaurant, we tried to buy the property next door to make an extension, but the person trying to sell it didn't actually own it.

I am not sure I would want to cope with the British weather full-time again but there are plenty of things I miss about Britain

He had some papers, which at first sight looked okay, but they weren't correct. It was lucky that we had a sharp *gestor*, who spotted it. So when transacting business here you really need to employ somebody fluent in the language and qualified in their field.

Something that struck me recently which might also be a disadvantage to living here is that I think I have become less tolerant of certain types of British people, including those with strong accents. That is ironic in a way because I have a noticeable Merseyside accent. I think I have also become snobby, perhaps as a reaction against a certain type of aggressive, over-Britishness which you find in some people here: they become 'professional' Londoners, Scousers, Mancunians, etc. My tolerance of that has definitely reduced, probably because I don't want to be lumped in with them. Perhaps that is why I think I sometimes overcompensate with the Spanish mothers at school and am overkeen to show that I speak some Spanish and fit in.

I think that many Spanish people are pretty tolerant and accepting of the foreigners in their country, possibly more so than they used to be. But I find that I have to make the effort to approach Spanish mothers at school and speak to them. You have to persevere if you want to integrate with Spanish people, whereas with other foreigners here it is easier. As well as the shared language of English, there is a sort of Dunkirk spirit which draws people together. I have only got one close Spanish friend. She doesn't speak much English but she is an Anglophile and is sending her children to private English lessons. I met her because our children are friends, which is how we have met a lot of the people we know here.

Open Minds

I would be happy to return to live in Britain, which I think is a great country, and we always look forward to going back there on holiday. But we didn't leave in the first place because we didn't like it, but to try a new life in a relaxed place, which we have done. I am not sure I would want to cope with the British weather full-time again but there are plenty of things I miss about Britain. Everything seems to be easier there, not just because of the language. You can get things done more quickly and efficiently and the facilities are better – for example, shopping centres where you can get everything under one roof – although things like that are better here now than they used to be. We also miss the salaries you can earn in Britain. We are doing okay now but it has taken time and we don't earn as much as I had thought we would.

If you are serious about moving here full time, you need to learn at least basic Spanish before you come and keep it up after you arrive. It makes things so much easier and the locals appreciate the effort. You also need to take advice about good legal representatives – lawyers and *gestors* – and use them for all legal and financial matters. They are crucial to protect your interests. And if you are planning to start a business here, do loads of research first about all aspects of it. We did quite a lot, but we also relied on others, and I wish we had done more ourselves.

missing people at home puts some people off moving abroad, but you might actually see more of your family and friends here than you did before

But if it is right for you, do it. You can have a nice life here. But try to work out if you would take to it before actually coming. I feel that I am the sort of person who can make my home anywhere, as long as I live near an airport or station. But not everybody is like that. Listen to advice about moving here but don't necessarily be put off by what others might say. For example, one of my relatives said something like, "What a waste. What was the point of going to university?" But that missed the point entirely: going to university was one of the things that opened my mind to the possibilities we have these days, of different ways of living our life.

Missing people at home puts some people off moving abroad, but you might actually find that you see more of your family and friends here than you did back in the UK, especially if you lived away from home in the UK. If they come over to Spain once or twice a year and you go back once or twice, you might see them solidly for about a month, but in UK if you only saw them for the odd weekend every now and then, you would see them less overall. That might be a good or a bad thing!

Short & Mostly Sweet

Londoner Jim Drury spent fourteen months living and
working in Benalmadena, where he was employed by
an expatriate newspaper. When things didn't work
out, he was glad he hadn't burned his bridges.

I came to Spain because I was looking to have a break from England. It was impossible to get work in Canada, where I was first looking, so a friend suggested that I get a job on one of the Costa del Sol's expatriate newspapers, which seemed to be a sound idea. The location appealed to me because it was near enough to pop back to Britain regularly and also gave me the chance to live in a country with a more European culture than I enjoyed in Britain. The offer of a job was the catalyst. I found employment before I arrived by sending my CV to every English-language publication on the Costa del Sol. Within three weeks, I had been offered a job and had moved out to Spain.

Hitting The Bottom

I found the first six weeks very difficult indeed. I didn't know anybody in Spain before I came and it took me some time to find a group of friends, especially as most of the people I worked with at the time were Spanish and I couldn't speak their language. Because it was winter when I arrived, the town in which I lived was very quiet and the bars in which I drank were almost empty. The only thing that stopped me from returning to England was the sense of failure that I would have experienced had I done so.

As an expat who returned to Blighty within eighteen months of moving to Spain, and at the risk of sounding patronising – I am going to offer some words of caution regarding the pitfalls of the monumental move you are about to make. There are two things you really must not do. Firstly, don't move here because you enjoy a fortnight's sunbathing in Torremolinos and fancy an extended vacation drinking large gin and tonics. Most Brits in Spain work long hours for low pay to make ends meet and, even for those with savings, life can be hard.

Secondly, don't come here because you are running away from an unhappy situation in your life, be it a broken marriage or the collapse of a business venture. Lots of people move to Spain as a means of escape from an unpalatable situation at home. Almost as many go running back with their tail between their legs – and a far lighter wallet.

Planning is vital. Like many of my compatriots who emigrate to Spain, I failed to plan my move as thoroughly as I would have done had I been less desperate to leave the UK. Having spent just one week in the country – two decades earlier as a nine-year-old – I decided on a whim to apply for jobs in the English-language media on the Costa del Sol. After seven years working as a journalist in Britain I had hit a brick wall in both my career and personal life and wanted some time out to get my head together. See what I mean about running away from things?

Within three weeks of the idea germinating in my brain, I was sitting in an office overlooking the mountains, writing copy and drinking *tinto de verano* (a mixture of red wine and lemonade or soda) into the early hours. Despite the beauty of my surroundings, I found the first two months excruciatingly hard. Arriving alone on 1st November, just when the coast had emptied of the last of the year's holidaymakers, I moved into a flat in the middle of what had overnight become a ghost town.

> *within seconds they both picked up their drinks and moved to another table. I had never felt so alone*

At first I found making friends difficult, and the idea of getting a girlfriend was frankly laughable. I was the only Briton in my office and, due to the language barrier separating me from my colleagues, I was desperately lonely. Friday nights were hell. I would get to my flat at six o'clock at night and wonder how on earth I was going to fill my time until the alarm rang on Monday morning.

More often than not, during those early weekends, I would find a sparsely-populated British pub and sit on my own, drinking myself into a semi-stupor and hoping for any form of conversation, however short. The lowest point came when I visited the pub below my flat one night when it was staging some typically bad Costa cabaret. I plonked myself next to two guys and started a conversation. Within seconds they both picked up their drinks and moved to another table. I had never felt so alone.

Facing Reality

Thankfully I didn't throw in the towel, and things improved when a group of British people in an adjoining office to mine took me under their wing. To those wonderful people I am eternally grateful. One couple, in particular, invited me into their circle of Spanish friends and introduced me to the local culture.

There are many negatives to staying inside the bubble of a parochial expat community. It is a synthetic, unreal place to live and can easily stifle your desire to explore the real Spain. But it is also a warm and comforting place to be and, without the encouragement and support of the many expats I befriended, my trip would have been over almost before it had begun.

The Brits on the Costa del Sol were an extraordinary mix of people. For good or ill, many expatriates reinvent themselves upon their arrival, recreating colourful and grandiose former careers and escapades. From the eccentric old soaks ravaging their livers for eight hours a day with obscene measure of spirits to the 'little bit whoah, little bit whey' sub-criminal element, I met an incredible array of people.

I didn't find the much maligned Spanish red tape and baffling bureaucracy to be too bad because a woman I worked with had very good local official contacts, which enabled me to get my *NIE* number pretty easily. Then again, before I met her, I had encountered appalling morning queuing in the local police office when trying to get the same *NIE* number. It was like a scene from hell, with Spanish officials screaming at anyone who had the wrong form, including me. I queued for three hours and wondered what on earth I was doing in Spain. But having a job in which I paid my dues out of my wages meant that I was free from the worst excesses of bureaucracy.

Surprisingly, I found it impossible to find a flat on a long let. As a result, I stayed in six flats in the fourteen months I lived in Spain.

The biggest regret of my Spanish adventure was not learning the language. Due to the impulsive nature of my move, I had no time to start lessons before my departure from London and to my eternal shame abandoned my attempts to speaka da lingo almost as soon as I had ordered my first *café con leche* (milky coffee).

> **I fell in love with the Spanish people and their way of living, and have tried to take a slice of that back with me**

Therefore, when I walked out of my job in Spain – rather elegantly I thought, having been repeatedly called the rudest word in the Oxford dictionary by my remarkably charming, slim, classy boss – I was in a quandary. Without the ability to speak Spanish there was little chance of other work in the media and I was faced with a stark choice: pull pints behind a bar, walk the streets selling real estate, or go back home.

The Best Of Spanish

I chose the latter and am pleased to say made the right decision. Fortunately, I had rented out my house in London instead of selling it, so was able to pick up life in England without difficulty. A year after my return to the UK, I look back on my Spanish voyage with great affection and very few regrets. I met many interesting people from all walks of life and have made some fantastic friends for life. First and foremost, I fell in love with the Spanish people and their way of living, and have tried to take a slice of that lifestyle and mentality back with me to London.

My advice to anyone mulling over such a move is: "Don't put all your eggs in one basket." A cliché, I know, but worth bearing in mind, all the same. Think very carefully before selling your home in England and ploughing the money into a business here. If you can afford to, keep hold of your property in the UK and rent it out. By doing so, you will have a fall-back position should your dream go sour.

Prepare your move sensibly and, whatever happens, you will have a life-shaping experience without ruining a lifetime's hard work in the blink of any eye. If you decide to go ahead with the move, try to enjoy the culture of this wonderful country and take advantage of everything it has to offer.

I implore you not to take the easy option of being a 'little Englander' with no sense of adventure outside frequenting John Bull pubs and fish and chip shops. There are plenty of those back home, even if you can't wear shorts for ten months of the year there.

To recap, my recommended ingredients are as follows: one healthy sense of adventure, a dash of caution, a large dollop of preparation, and a good measure of hard work. Stir well and you might just have created the recipe for a happy expatriate life.

I wish you the best of British!

Cutting And Running

Tracey Hastwell left Manchester, England
for Los Boliches in search of sun, sea and sand.
Seventeen years — and several boyfriends — later,
she found that her priorities had changed.

I wanted to try life in Spain because I was young, had no ties and liked the sun, sea and sand which it offered, all of them rare in Manchester. Going out was very cheap in Spain then and I was at an age (24) when I wanted to party every night, which definitely isn't the case now. I chose Los Boliches for no reason other than that my mum and dad had bought an apartment there. Isn't life so much simpler when you're young?

A Tale Of Three Boyfriends

I found settling into life in Spain very easy, but I was young and had no responsibilities, and that makes it much easier to adapt. And I didn't actually think about the fact that it was different living in Spain, although it certainly was. It helped that I found it easy to make friends. In fact, on my first night in the country, I met a Spaniard, José, who became my boyfriend for a year. I didn't speak a word of Spanish back then and he had no English, but I was with a girlfriend who spoke a little Spanish and she translated for us.

That started me learning the language immediately and by the time we split up a year later, I spoke it quite well; that helps the settling-in process enormously and is also of great practical help. I split up with José because he began to feel guilty about not having told me that he was actually married with two kids, and so he confessed! He worked as an engineer on a fairground that was open at night, which was why he was able to see me in the evenings. But he actually lived in Malaga with his family.

I met my next boyfriend, Pedro, about six months later, and went out with him for ten years. He worked in the family bar and only spoke 'bar English' when we met, meaning he could take drinks orders and talk about the weather, but not much else. For the first two years of our relationship we spoke just Spanish, which meant that I became a good speaker, and that really helps you to settle in.

Having a mobile skill like hairdressing also helped. There will always be work, you can operate anywhere, and being able to work at something that you already know helps you to settle into a new place. For the first year, however, I did mainly bar work, but that was easy to find and also a good way of meeting people. And I cut hair in some of the bars as a sideline!

My only experience of learning Spanish is by learning through having a Spanish partner. I don't think it is a particularly difficult language to learn, although there are some Spaniards who I never learned to understand. Even after a decade, I couldn't understand much of what Pedro's dad said. Like a lot of older people, he used old-fashioned words for things, words that have fallen out of use. That and his accent sometimes made it impossible to understand what he was saying.

It helps the learning process if you don't mind getting things wrong, because you will get a lot wrong at the start. Some Spanish words have totally different meanings just by having an accent over one letter, so you can easily say something completely different to what you mean. People laughed at me a lot at first, but not in a bad way.

> *if you have more than one drink, you are seen as an alcoholic; more than a couple of fags, and you're a druggie*

I don't really think Spanish men and British women are compatible, which might sound odd after having gone out with one of them for ten years. But the British and Spanish are brought up differently and the cultures are quite different too. You don't notice the differences at first – during the first flush of the romance – but then they begin to come out.

I think one of the main things is that quite a lot of Spanish people have a straightforward, almost simple view of life. If the men have a nice wife at home, a steady job and reasonable health, they are happy and don't think they should ask for more from life. I remember Pedro saying to me something like 'ambition kills'. But I think we are generally more ambitious than the Spanish – certainly the Andalusian Spanish – and want more variety from life, meaning that we are more adventurous, which can cause problems in a relationship.

And Spanish people, both men and women, can seem quite possessive to us. They don't really like their partners going out without them. If you, as a woman, go out in a group without your man, and there are men in the group, he can get really stroppy. It isn't really the done thing. I went into Pedro's bar once with several friends, some of them men, and he went spare, but it hadn't occurred to me that it would be a problem. And some Spanish men can get a bit funny about women smoking and drinking in public. If you have more than one drink, you are seen as an alcoholic; more than a couple of fags, and you're a druggie. And it isn't just me who has found this. Lots of my English girlfriends have had problems with their Spanish husbands and boyfriends.

But I think the most common problem is boredom. The men are solid enough and provide for their families, but they haven't got much 'get up and go' and they want to do the same things all the time. It is like a routine. They go out for lunch every Sunday, for example, often with the same people, and to the same beach bar or restaurant. And the annual holiday is taken at the same time every year, in the same resort, usually at the same hotel or apartment. It is usually in Spain, of course, on one of the Costas, or Tenerife if they are a bit more adventurous.

I also think you miss the banter if you aren't a native Spanish speaker and your boyfriend isn't a native English speaker. You can communicate well enough when you reach a certain level with each other's languages, but quick-fire banter never really quite happens. I noticed that immediately when I started seeing Darren, who is English.

As for my view of Spanish people in general, I have come to the conclusion that quite a few of them think they are special. It might be because they are idolised so much as kids and really put on a pedestal. So they are used to getting what they want, straight away. That probably explains why they don't like queuing and drive with little or no regard for anybody else on the road.

I think the Spanish opinion of foreigners has changed quite a lot over the time I have been here. When I arrived in 1987, we were much more of a novelty and generally were liked. But there are so many more foreigners here now and the Spanish sometimes think that they have been taken over, which isn't an unreasonable opinion. But they have some strange views about foreigners. For a start, they seem to lump us all together, whatever our nationality. And some Spaniards seem to think that we don't work but just sponge off the state, which certainly isn't true. Foreigners seem to be able to do that in Britain, but they certainly can't here.

> *I now realise that it was probably a subtle way of asking for a bribe*

And I think some Spanish women regard foreign women as a threat, especially if they have a Spanish boyfriend, so I have never really made any Spanish girlfriends. Even Pedro's sister didn't say more than hello and goodbye to me during the first couple of years of our relationship, although we all went out to dinner regularly. I think she saw me as a funny foreigner and that the relationship wouldn't last, so I wasn't worth getting to know.

But I do sympathise with Spaniards who don't really like or approve of us. I have seen a lot of Brits who don't have much of a clue about life here and make no effort to adapt or fit in. They somehow imagine that it is going to be easy living in Spain, like one long holiday. The younger ones flit from low-paid job to low-paid job, with little thought about the future, while the retirees don't do anything with their lives, except drink too much. Obviously, not everybody here is like that, but a fair amount of people are.

Bribery & Corruption

I don't think setting up and running a business in Spain are as difficult as people sometimes say. The crucial thing is to get a good lawyer and accountant. If you have them, they will sort everything out for you. But you have to be careful about who you employ. When I started the business, I had a problem with a lawyer. I paid him to arrange for all the papers I needed to start the hairdressing salon, but when the police came round to check my papers, I found out that the lawyer had done hardly any of the work, despite having been paid for it.

But it got more complex. The police asked me to pay for an advert for the salon in an internal police magazine, which sounded odd. I now realise that it was probably a subtle way of asking for a bribe not to follow up on the fact that I didn't have all the necessary papers. I was naïve at the time and didn't realise, so I said no. A week later the police returned and ordered me to report to the station the next day. I nearly got deported and it was only because I employed another very good (Argentinian) lawyer that the situation got sorted out.

That was prior to 1992, when Spain joined the EU; the process for opening a business is easier now, but you still have to be careful. And I think I might now have some recourse against the original lawyer who didn't do his job. There was none then. So I would strongly recommend that people ask around and make sure they get a lawyer and accountant with proven track records with people whose opinion they trust, although that is sometimes easier said than done.

Other things to remember are that social security contributions are very high in Spain for self-employed people, although you do get a pension out of it. And it is expensive to employ staff and can be difficult to dismiss them without paying a fortune in compensation. As well as paying their wages and social security – twice a year, in June and December – as part of a standard work contract, you also have to pay them double wages. And once they have worked for you for a certain time, it is expensive to get rid of them, however rubbish they are. And there are plenty like that. In fact, the strength of workers' rights in Spain is seen as holding back the economy, because employers are reluctant to employ staff on proper contracts. And this of course encourages the black economy, which is strong in this country.

Property Problems

When I arrived in Spain, I rented property and did so for some years. It was a lot more casual then: there were often no contracts and you didn't have to pay two or three months upfront as is required now. And it used to be very cheap, but prices have rocketed in the last couple of years. The main warning I would give to anybody, whether renting or buying in Spain, is to beware of the noise problem.

Spain can be a very noisy country and, if you live next to some lively locals or to a place that is rented out to rowdy holidaymakers, life can be very difficult. You will notice this especially if you are used to living in a house in England and move to a flat in Spain. A major problem is that Spanish flats often aren't soundproofed properly, or at all. If you are unlucky, you can be disturbed from above, below and both sides. Perhaps even from the outside too.

The Spanish are naturally very loud and keep very different hours from us, particularly during the warmer months, and you might find that your neighbours stay up half the night, keeping you awake. This can be very distressing, especially if you have come out here for a quiet retirement.

As for buying, I have done that once. Getting the mortgage was straightforward enough because I had a good accountant and he sorted it out. We bought 'off plan', which means buying before the property is built. You pay only small amounts as it is being built and these secure your rights to the property – provided that you come up with the full payments upon completion, of course. A lot of people have done well out of buying off plan, because in the recent rising market, prices have shot up in the year or two that it takes to build the properties, so the buyers make a good profit for little up-front investment.

But we have had a real problem with our building and this isn't uncommon. The first thing was the timeframe. Construction dragged on for a year longer than it should have done. Some delay is usual but a year is a lot. It really messes you around, especially if you have to arrange for a place to rent while you are waiting. But the worst thing has been the very poor nature of the finish on the building.

The builders were so bad that the owners in the building have banded together to take them to court. They completely failed to build a sauna and gym as promised in the plans, the building has very bad damp problems when it rains and they didn't build the interior walls as they should have done, meaning that noise really carries between the different apartments. In addition, we had a long crack on the terrace, which kept getting wider. The builders said that they would sort it out when the building 'had settled', but I wonder if it will fall on someone first. I also know of at least six apartments which have flooded because the builders apparently used inferior plumbing parts on the sinks and some have burst. So you do take something of a gamble in agreeing to buy a property before it is built, because you can't pre-check the quality of the workmanship.

Floods & Phones

Spain has changed a great deal in my seventeen years in the country. When I arrived, Los Boliches still had the feeling of a fishing village, but there has been so much building since then that the scale of the place has been transformed. That is common all along the coast and I think it feels claustrophobic now. Having said that, it is a lot more geared towards foreigners now and you can get just about anything you want without going far. It used to be a big thing with Brits to trek to Gibraltar to stock up on British goodies, but you don't need to do that now.

But I don't feel as safe here as I used to do. Even as a woman on my own I didn't used to think twice about walking around town late at night, but that has changed, along with the type of people you find living on the Costa del Sol. I feel threatened by some of the Moroccan men and other Africans who have moved here and I know of other women who feel the same. In fact, there is increasing bad feeling between Europeans and Africans.

many is the time I have had to try to finish somebody's hair by candlelight

Another thing that has changed is the weather. That might sound silly but it definitely has. It has got more extreme. The summers are hotter and more humid, and the winters are colder and wetter. When it rains here, it has always rained hard, as it does in the tropics, but that seems to have got worse too. And it can be very destructive. The drains in the salon often used to back up during heavy rain, because the main drains couldn't cope. We used to get flooded – and not just by water. Imagine trying to run a business when you are worrying about swilling the sewage out of the salon! The electricity cables in the walls also used to get damp during the rain and we would have power cuts. Many is the time I have had to try to finish somebody's hair by candlelight. But if you are in the middle of something that needs power – a blow-dry, for example – you just have to wait for the power to come back. It's all a bit primitive really.

We have just had a problem with Telefonica, the national telephone company, which is famous – or infamous – for being difficult to deal with. That said, they aren't as bad as they used to be. People sometimes used to have to wait, literally, for years, to have a telephone line installed.

A couple of months ago we started to hear other voices on the line. We assumed at first that it was a crossed line, but it persisted and it turned out that Telefonica had given our number to the bloke across the road, as a temporary measure while they were trying to get him a number! They had apparently 'run out of numbers'. You couldn't make this up, could you? And whose bill were the calls supposed to go on, with the 'shared' number? Ours or his? He is Iranian, by the way, and speaks five languages, so he regularly makes calls all over the world, so who knows what his bill is like!

Anyway, even though the chap across the road had specifically told us that Telefonica had given him our number, when we rang them to complain, they persistently denied it, insisting that it was a crossed line. It took ten phone calls for them to send an engineer round. At first he too insisted it was a crossed line. We sorted it out eventually, but only after a couple of months of hassle and worry. And I don't know how somebody who doesn't speak decent Spanish as I do would manage.

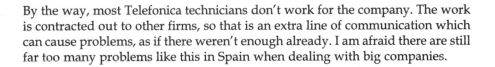

don't imagine that working here is the same as in the UK; the wages are low and you will have few, if any, rights

By the way, most Telefonica technicians don't work for the company. The work is contracted out to other firms, so that is an extra line of communication which can cause problems, as if there weren't enough already. I am afraid there are still far too many problems like this in Spain when dealing with big companies.

Needing A Change

Most people's reaction in Spain to news of our return to the UK has been one of surprise and to ask, "Why ever do you want to go back?" I think it is partly because a lot of people won't admit to themselves that life in Spain is anything less than perfect. In fact, I think a lot of foreigners here say they are happy when they aren't really. They don't want to hear something which reminds them that they might have problems and concerns – and somebody leaving Spain focuses their minds on those.

When we start to explain why we don't want to stay in Spain, people's attitudes tend to soften and they sometimes agree with our reservations about living here. The main reason for the return is that my fiancé Darren, who is an electrician, can't make a decent living here, as a lot of people find. Don't imagine that working here is the same as in the UK. The wages are low and you will have few, if any, rights, unless you have a contract, and they aren't always easy to get.

As for me, I simply need a change after being here for so long. I have seen a lot of Spain and lived the lifestyle here and it is time to move on. Besides that, when you have your own business, you spend most of the time working and don't get a lot of chance to take advantage of the good things here – and there are good things as well as bad. Your expectations change as you get older and I want more than to live in a warm, laid-back place where not much happens.

We have also found that it is ever more difficult to make close friends because people come and go with increasing rapidity. And I have had enough of the red tape, the crazy driving, the *mañana* syndrome and the fact that prices have gone up so much since the introduction of the euro.

If somebody asked for my advice about moving to Spain, I would first say, "Really do your homework." If you have children, think carefully about how the move will affect them. The younger they are, the easier they will find it to adapt. I don't have kids but friends who do are generally impressed by the education system here, although there is some bullying of foreign kids and older British children sometimes find learning the language really hard. I know of one thirteen-year-old who has been left behind by the language, even though he has been here for two years.

Really ask yourself why you are coming here. If it is just for the weather and a relaxed time, that is not enough – because living in Spain is often not relaxed and you will have little time to enjoy the weather because you will be working. I have noticed that people in Britain who are thinking of moving to Spain idealise it. I am often asked for advice and, when I explain what it is actually like, with the disadvantages as well as the advantages, people are usually surprised. They had thought it was all sweetness and light. It isn't – but then nowhere is.

Deliverance

Patrick Hickey and Wicki Thomson gave up an all-consuming lifestyle running their own businesses in Denmark in order to bring up their son, Daniel, on the Costa del Sol. It wasn't the ideal choice.

Our Spanish adventure began in Denmark in December 1996, when my wife Wicki gave birth to our son Daniel. Neither of us were spring chickens by then: she was forty, while I had reached the grand old age of forty-two, and Daniel was a much wanted child. His arrival turned our lives upside down, but in a very positive way. We had been running a rather successful small group of companies, involved in areas ranging from computers to organising rock and jazz group tours and festivals, and some of our clients were international household names (I am far too modest to name any of them).

The disadvantage of successful businesses, however, is that they usually require constant attention in order to keep them successful, so we had been used to a twenty-four hours per day, seven days per week work life. We quickly discovered that this was incompatible with being the type of parents we longed to be and it was an obvious and easy decision to put the companies up for sale and opt for retirement so that we could devote ourselves to our son full time.

So we sold the companies and then began to think about where to retire. We first considered the South of France and were happy with the location, but then my uncle Allan and aunt Dagny intervened and began to convince us that southern Spain was where we should head for.

Second Time Lucky

Having lived on the Costa del Sol for a quarter of a century and built up a very successful property business, they were in an excellent position to give us the low-down on every aspect of life here. They were also there to offer help and advice if required. They did a very good job of selling the region to us, and it was probably two things that really swayed our decision from southern France to southern Spain: the climate and low cost of living on the Costa del Sol (although the latter has increased somewhat since the mid-1990s). Since moving here, we have found other factors that have convinced us that it was the correct decision.

> *if you think that the Andalusians on the coast have a laid-back attitude, they are positively stressed out compared with the folks here*

Around seven months after speaking to my uncle and aunt about where to retire to, we bought a plot in Mijas Costa on the Costa del Sol and arranged to have a house built on it. We moved to Spain in May 1998, rented a house in Fuengirola while the house was being finished and moved in five months later. And there we were, living in just the type of house that we wanted, enjoying stunning views of the Mijas mountains and Mijas village.

We spent four great years there and made a lot of close friends of various nationalities, but we had made one quite serious mistake in choosing the plot and building our house: the house was facing north and it put the terrace and swimming pool in the shade during the winter months, which is the time when you want to maximise the amount of sun you receive. So life there could become rather gloomy for around a third of the year. That was one reason we wanted to move. There had also been a crazy rise in local property prices in the intervening four years and we wanted to cash in on that; we ended up getting ourselves a pretty good deal.

We decided to look for a place situated slightly inland, in a region where prices were still to rise as severely as they had along much of the coast. We looked at several locations in the country and mountains behind both the western and eastern Costa del Sol, and stumbled across a lovely twelve-year-old *finca* (a rural property, usually with land) in the *campo* (countryside) outside the town of Cómpeta (a mountain town inland from Torre del Mar on the eastern Costa del Sol), which we bought and are very happy in.

The process of buying property is rather different from Denmark, but we haven't had many problems. When we had the house built on Mijas Costa, the builder sorted out all the practical and financial matters and so it was very easy for us. The only hurdle we had was a delay in finishing, which is common here. The wait for our house to be completed was long, almost six months, but we made the best of the situation by using the time to hit the road and explore the whole of Andalusia.

Buying our present house was very straightforward, but the associated paperwork took an age to be completed. For example, although we bought the house in June 2002, we didn't receive the final papers for our water contract until May 2004.

The Country & The Coast

Our 'eyrie' is 650 metres above the waters of the Mediterranean, which look particularly blue and sparkling from up here. Unfortunately, when you are actually next to the Med or in the water, it tends to be brown, sludgy and a health hazard, with things floating in it that it is best not to speculate about.

We have never regretted our move to Cómpeta and life up here is certainly different from that on the coast. In fact, there is a completely different attitude to life. If you think that the Andalusians on the coast have a laid-back attitude, they are positively stressed out compared with the folks here. Life is much more relaxed in this part of the world and partying is much more frequent, while the coast has become busier and more hectic over recent years, more city-like, serious and frenetic. And hordes and hordes of people now live there.

Communities in the mountains are invariably still smaller than those on the coast. Everything up here is on a scale that seems easier to handle, which we really enjoy. The contacts you have with the locals and your general interaction with people seem to be far more relaxed, and this even extends to dealings with the local authorities. They tend to have a more understanding attitude than the authorities on the coast, even with regard to the language barrier. Whereas the police on the coast will insist that you come with a translator if you need one, here the police are quite likely to go out and find one for you among the local community. It's a nice way of doing things.

I suppose the contrast between life here and life on the coast is comparable with the difference between rural and urban life back in Denmark. The first is more small-scale, relaxed, quirky and friendly, and people have more time for each other, more patience. I cannot think of many disadvantages of living here. There is less shopping available (although some people see this as a benefit), but the large coastal supermarkets are only a half-hour drive away, and in an hour you can be in the centre of Malaga, a city of around 600,000 people, with an international airport, so we are hardly living in the back of beyond. Nevertheless, some of my coastal friends kid us that the community we live in is like something out of the Burt Reynolds film Deliverance. Do I hear a banjo playing in the background and see somebody marrying his sister, and why do I keep saying "My, my, boy, you've got a pretty mouth" in an American country halfwit accent?

Words Of Advice

Plenty of foreigners still seem to be coming to Spain to start new lives. They come for all sorts of reasons and from many different backgrounds, so it is difficult to give advice which covers all circumstances, but to those who are considering it, I can offer some general words based on our experiences.

First, you will find it much easier to integrate if you learn the language. Contrary to what some people say, however, you don't have to become an expert and be able to debate the finer points of existentialist philosophy (if there are any), but you should try to learn enough to conduct a basic conversation. A lot of Spaniards can speak English (as can Danes!), but once your neighbours discover that you are willing and able to speak some Spanish (and the fact that you are trying is at least as important as your ability, or lack of it), doors will open everywhere. You will find that this applies particularly in smaller mountain communities like ours rather than on the busier, more anonymous coast.

Next, try to build relationships with Spanish people as well as with other foreigners. At first acquaintance, I think that some Spaniards can appear quite reserved, but if you try to communicate a few times, they often open up and we have never had any negative experiences. As an aid to making friends with Spanish people, do some research into the history and background of Spain: there are plenty of good books available. A bit of background knowledge will give you an understanding of why the locals do things the way that they do and why the laws are sometimes so complicated and seemingly illogical. Reading up on the subject will also help you to appreciate the development of the local culture.

some things take a hell of a long time to get done, but they usually do get done, eventually, in one form or another

If you intend to stay in Spain for a long time, try to get involved in local activities. Contact the town hall and other local authorities and groups: help is always wanted with local projects, for example bartending or cleaning at local ferias, or assisting with old people and educational courses. It is a good way to make friends, integrate into the community and build up local contacts. Plenty of local municipalities put up posters which encourage local foreigners to participate in local affairs, including voting: the politicians have noticed that we are here in numbers and they want our votes! I think it is easier to get involved in the community in smaller mountain towns than it is in the large, rapidly merging urban sprawls on the coast.

Another recommendation is to accustom yourself to the way the authorities work in this part of the world. Or rather, to accustom yourself to the slowness at which they work, or the fact that they sometimes don't work at all! Even the seemingly simplest thing can sometimes become very complicated and difficult to transact in Andalusia, and for no obvious reasons. Some things take a hell of a long time to get done, but they usually do get done, eventually, in one form or another. Learning to accept this, or at least to not be too hassled by it, is an important part of settling into life in southern Spain.

The following story demonstrates the particular methods that Spanish people sometimes employ to do things. These methods can appear strange to us foreigners but, if you want to make a go of things here, it is important to learn to accept them, or at least to put up with them.

Mystery In The Mountains

One afternoon a couple of years ago, I received a phone call from a Spaniard. I didn't understand everything he said, but I picked up the fact that there was a parcel waiting for me in the Bar Bella Vista in the small town of Algarrobo down on the coast, twenty kilometres away. This made no sense whatsoever, but I decided that it was my fault for not understanding the phone call properly.

perhaps the package contained a bomb, or a huge wad of cash or bags of drugs

As I was beginning to forget about it a quarter of an hour later, the phone went again and this time there was an Englishman's voice at the other end. He explained that he lived in Algarrobo and the bar owner had asked him to ring me to clarify what had been said in the earlier phone call. I hadn't been mistaken and he repeated that there was a parcel for me in the bar. He gave me instructions how to reach the place and said to ask for the bar owner, Pepe, when I arrived.

I wondered what was going on. At this early stage of our life in Cómpeta, only close family members and a few local officials knew our address, let alone the telephone number. For the next couple of hours, Wicki and I wondered whether it was a practical joke. And then my mind turned to darker possibilities. Although I am Danish, my name is very Irish sounding, so I began to wonder about terrorists and mistaken identity. Perhaps the package contained a bomb, or a huge wad of cash or bags of drugs.

After much thought, Wicki, Daniel and I took a drive down to Algarrobo and found the Bar Bella Vista. It was situated just across the road from a Guardia Civil (one of the three Spanish police forces) office, which cheered me up in view of the thoughts that had earlier been polluting my mind. While Wicki and Daniel stayed at a safe distance, I entered the bar alone and presented myself to the barman, who turned out to be the mysterious Pepe.

There was a bit of confusion on his part about who I was until I mentioned that somebody had called me, on his behalf, to explain the message about the package. His face broke into a grin and he fetched a large white envelope from behind the cash register. He handed it to me and asked if I would like a drink – on the house. My confusion deepened as I looked at the envelope and saw my name, address and telephone number on it. Even odder, it was an official DHL envelope and had come from Denmark.

I turned down the kind offer of the drink, returned to the family and opened the envelope a safe distance from the car, because thoughts of Ian Fleming and John Le Carré plots were still in my mind. What I found was commonplace: a letter from Diner's Club and my renewed corporate and private credit cards. The credit card companies send their cards by courier for greater security (at some expense, I imagine), but that isn't much good if the local driver decides to save time by leaving the letter and the card holder's telephone number with a complete stranger at a bar on the coast, to save himself a forty-kilometre round-trip up mountain roads!

Simple Tourists

As keen observers of our fellow foreigners in Spain, it seems to us that they can be divided into three sub-groups: tourists, short-termers and full-timers.

The average tourist is a simple beast, who saves his or her euros or kroner or pounds and arrives pale, plump and all-too-often empty-headed on the Spanish coast, armed and ready to be a spectator rather than a participant. Such people are often decent, sensible and perhaps even intelligent when in their own country, but they seem to leave their brains in a warehouse at the home airport before flying to Spain. Do they perhaps imagine that the heat in this country will melt their little grey cells?

The average tourist might pay lip service to seeing something genuinely Spanish when here and might make a nodding acquaintance with a bit of tourist flamenco or a donkey ride in a tourist trap, but apart from this, most are only after sun, sea, sand, sex (if they're lucky) and, most of all, cheap booze and cigarettes.

Unfortunately, the majority of Costa tourists show little or no respect for or interest in the locals. An obvious example is when you see a group waddling into a restaurant, clad only in swimming trunks or bikinis. You don't have to overdress here in order to eat out, but the minimum expected is a pair of shorts and a T-shirt in all restaurants except the *chiringuitos* (beachfront bars and restaurants), where bathing costumes are sometimes acceptable.

Spanish people don't make a fuss about such foreigner *faux pas*, but they do see it as an insulting lack of respect – and it gives them a disdain for tourists in general, although they are pragmatic enough to realise that these strange, loud, simple people are the bread and butter of the local economy.

Short-Term Or Full-Time?

Short-termers come to live in Spain for three or four years at most. They are becoming very numerous and originate from more and more countries, particularly since the expansion of the EU. Short-term foreigners can be divided into two groups: those who are legally registered and those who aren't, the latter sometimes also called 'adventurers'. These adventurers are very bad for the reputation of foreigners in Spain and colour the impression that the Spanish have of us, almost always negatively.

These are the people who drive cars from their home country, meaning that they pay no local car taxes and often have invalid insurance because the law requires you to change to Spanish plates and register your car after a certain length of time in Spain. They often get by doing odd jobs, all cash in hand, and send their kids to the local schools for free, because they don't pay taxes.

Such people are looked down on by the Spanish, interestingly not so much because of the tax evasion (Spain is a country where ignoring the rules isn't only expected but also admired), but because these people stick completely to their own community, only ever working for or becoming friends with other Danes, Britons or whoever. It is this isolationist behaviour that the Spanish object to. Why come here, they think, if you make not the slightest effort to fit in? The local perception is that if you are, say, British, you will usually have a British plumber, electrician, gardener, cleaner, etc, always sticking to your own. And maybe as many as eighty per cent of these foreign workers won't be registered.

The Spanish rarely get involved with people who they think are only here short term, for the sensible reason that it isn't worth investing the mental energy and emotions in getting to know people who will quite likely disappear overnight within a few months. They don't tend to feel animosity towards these fly-by-nights, so much as indifference. We have had similar experiences of getting to know people who, after a mere year or two, decide to move their 'tent' back to the home country or on somewhere else. We sit back, sad to have lost friends but undamaged by it. It is different, however, for our seven-year-old, because children sometimes feel these losses much more deeply than adults.

The full-timers, whether here to work or retire, are our favourite foreigners – those like us, of course! They have by far the best chance of integrating properly into Spanish life, but since you aren't required to sign a form stating your intention to stay in Spain long-term, it is difficult for the Spanish to identify us and hence decide whether to bother to get to know us. It therefore takes a few years for people like us to be taken seriously as long-term prospects, or 'local foreigners'.

A Big But Pleasant Surprise

Being the parents of a young child, one of our major concerns when we moved here was the quality of the healthcare; what would it really be like in a 'Latin' country? After six years in Andalusia, we know that any fears we had were unfounded – and we have quite extensive experience of healthcare upon which to base this opinion.

Our son has graced a Spanish emergency ward an impressive five times since we have been here. On one occasion, he was kicked by a donkey up in the Alpujarras (an isolated area of rugged mountains, inland from the eastern Costa del Sol) and the staff in the local emergency clinic decided that he needed treatment urgently in the large county hospital in Motril, which he received after an hour's ambulance ride. My mother-in-law spent two weeks in hospital in Torremolinos and, despite the language barrier, she was well cared for. But if you don't work in Spain and therefore pay into the social security system, you aren't covered by the health system and need to buy health insurance cover, which starts at around €550 per person per year, for which you get everything from general surgery to specialist treatment.

Living up in the mountains, we had wondered about access to emergency specialist medical treatment, as we are half an hour's drive from the nearest municipal hospital and at least an hour from the big hospitals in Malaga. But we don't have to worry because there are two helipads close to Cómpeta and the authorities don't hesitate to use them in emergencies. The helicopters are based in Malaga and arrive here within twenty minutes of a call.

> **the lack of regimentation
> and organisation is one of
> the things that attracts
> me to Andalusia**

So regarding healthcare, we can honestly say that we feel safer and better protected here than we did in Denmark, which has come as a big but pleasant surprise.

Many Benefits

When we lived on the coast, our son Daniel attended a public pre-school, where over half the pupils were foreigners. This was by no means ideal at a school that taught only in Spanish because around half of the class didn't understand Spanish and held the rest up. Daniel already spoke Spanish because he had been at a Spanish kindergarten. It is very different in Cómpeta because foreigners are very much in the minority – only around two or three per class – and the teachers have time to give them language tuition.

Overall, it appears to us that teachers in Andalusia seem more dedicated than their equivalents in Denmark, and our British friends think the same applies to education in Britain.

> *the only real cons are the bureaucracy and the obvious corruption, which is more a type of lifestyle than a symptom of a bent society*

The only thing we really miss about Denmark is family and friends. Some of the ways of doing things (or not doing them) in Spain can be frustrating, silly or outright stupid, and when I come across an example of that, I pine for the organisation of Denmark. But on the other hand, the lack of regimentation and organisation is one of the things that attracts me to Andalusia.

We enjoy our trips back to Denmark and have a lot of visitors from there, but apart from Wicki having the odd attack of sentimentality about the old country, we don't really miss it. And a five-day trip back usually cures her longing for all things Danish.

I would say that the pros of living here far outweigh the cons. The only real cons are the bureaucracy and also the obvious corruption, which is more a type of lifestyle than a symptom of a bent society. The benefits are many, including the excellent climate; the beauty of the sea, mountains and sky; living surrounded by nature; the low cost of living; a low crime rate; and a fascinating history, which is evident everywhere.

We intend to stay here at least until our son finishes his secondary education, which will be in 2012, and then we will reconsider our position and look at our options. Who knows what will have happened by then?

English As A Foreign Language

After 15 years in Spain, despite having a degree in
Spanish and European studies, a Spanish husband
and two bilingual daughters, Londoner Louise Scott
feels that in some ways she is still settling in.

I was instilled with a deep fascination and enthusiasm for Spain by my A Level Spanish teacher, so it was probably on the cards that I would come to live here. Visits to the country reaffirmed this enthusiasm and I think I literally fell in love with it. The decision to move here full-time came because of work: I was offered a job as an EFL (English as a Foreign Language) teacher. I decided to move to Granada because it was my favourite city. I had already lived in Spain for a short time, as part of my degree (in Spanish and European studies); during the third year, I spent about ten months in the country, three of them in Salamanca and seven in Granada.

Granada & Calahonda

Living in Granada was pretty different from living on the Costa del Sol (our current home is in Calahonda), partly because of the locals. The natives of Granada are regarded as offhand and cool by other Andalusians and are perhaps the most reserved people in the province. Their coolness is supposed to come from the snow on the nearby mountains. And there is a strange mix of people in the city: a strong, staid local middle class co-exists with the students from the university and quite a lot of hippy street entertainers, who come to entertain all the tourists. Granada is a year-round tourist destination, with endless streams of people coming to see the Alhambra, which is supposedly the most beautiful building in Europe. So the city tends to attract a more culture-seeking tourist than the coast.

The local middle class in Granada is quite parochial and difficult to penetrate but ironically seems to be more tolerant of foreigners than of other Spaniards. My husband is from Malaga, and they always seemed to try to make his life difficult. They also have quite a strange accent in Granada, which is more difficult to understand than the Malaga one. And Granada's climate is more extreme than the coast: hotter in summer and colder in winter, and that can be rather draining. I shouldn't complain too much, though; I met my husband in Granada!

Renting property is generally easy in Spain, but it was difficult to find somewhere in Granada – perhaps because of competition from the students – and all the flats I rented during my time there I found through friends and acquaintances rather than by adverts in the paper or through agents. That seems to be the case generally here in Spain, although I haven't rented for years.

The rental contracts I had in Granada were quite 'loose' and I think probably illegal since they didn't include any of the clauses they should. That is another feature of the Spanish rental market: it can be a bit casual, which is fine as long as everything goes well but can cause problems if there is conflict between landlord and tenant. However, I was a good tenant so I don't think the landlord ever needed to contemplate throwing me out.

One flat we rented (two other students and I) had no contract at all and at Christmas, while we were all away, the landlord and his family stayed at the flat without our permission. But we got a month's rent for free as compensation, after we had threatened to denounce him for not declaring rental income to the tax people! A word of warning about renting: getting the landlord to repair or replace faulty or broken items can be difficult, but I think that is the same everywhere.

As for buying property, I have bought three and I would say that the process is very easy but that is only because I have had a lawyer do it, which is crucial in order to protect your interests. Having a husband who is a lawyer obviously made things much easier. If you don't employ a lawyer, you probably won't understand the buying process or the implications of certain steps.

One aspect of buying and selling here that certainly gives you peace of mind is the fact that once the buyer has paid a deposit, there is no going back, so it is very unlikely that you will get caught out by a buyer pulling out. The only difficult thing I found in all three cases of buying was finding the money for all the expenses you have to pay on top of the actual house price – look to pay at least ten per cent extra for the transfer tax, etc.

 some Spaniards are surprised to discover that a British person can learn to speak Spanish

We have also had some experience of renovating a property in Spain. Our current house was only used for one month per year for around twenty years by the previous owner and so needed just about everything replacing or redoing. Unfortunately, we didn't have the funds to do the work before we moved in and so we have gradually done stuff over the years. The major piece of advice I would offer to people is that having the bathroom or kitchen done while you are living there is very stressful. All the work we have had done has taken longer than both we and the builder originally thought (often several weeks longer) and it has all cost more than originally estimated, but that is mainly because we have made changes or had extra things done.

All the renovation has been done by Spanish workmen (as you would expect, some have been better than others), except for some new windows, which we had put in by a British firm. I wouldn't recommend that you have a non-Spaniard do specialist jobs such as floor tiling, plumbing or electricity because locals are trained in these techniques. I have also noticed that non-Spanish workmen who don't speak Spanish seem to take longer to get materials because of the language barrier. They probably also have to pay more for them, which means you will have to as well.

Language & Legalities

Even though I have a degree in Spanish, there are still hurdles to learning the language fluently because the various accents in southern Spain can be difficult to understand and the speed at which people talk is another barrier. In Salamanca (a city to the north-west of Madrid) I understood everyone more or less perfectly, but when I arrived in Andalusia my confidence was completely crushed, as I found that I didn't understand a lot of what people said. For example, *resfriado* (a cold) is pronounced without the S and *fulgoneta* (a van) has an R in it instead of an L. After fifteen years, there are still people here I don't understand at all! However, my daughters translate for me.

There's a range of accents within the province – in Cordoba, Seville, Malaga and Granada. It is even worse in other regions, like Asturias, Galicia, Catalonia and Valencia, where you don't just have to contend with the local pronunciation of Castilian Spanish but also with the local language and/or dialect. I certainly don't want to put off anybody who is trying to learn Spanish, but even with a degree in the language and having a Spanish husband to talk to, I am still learning. And, interestingly, I have found that some Spaniards are surprised to discover that a British person can learn to speak Spanish! What does that say about our abilities with foreign tongues?

> *the Spanish are beginning to become indignant about the number of foreign children in the state schools*

It isn't easy running your own business in this country because it takes an age to really get anything off the ground, although the effort has been worth it. The main difficulty is that being self-employed or running your own business is very hard work and financially burdensome because of the tax and social security payments, which are nothing less than relentless. There is also a lot of red tape and I strongly recommend that people employ a *gestor* (a sort of cross between an administrator and a lawyer, but generally cheaper than the latter) to handle it, as we do. On top of this, we have found that officials rarely seem to remember us.

When I first came to the country, you had to have a visa from the Spanish consulate in order to qualify for a residence and work permit. I had to queue for hours on several occasions on London streets in order to get the visa stamp.

Once, in 1990, I had to get a new passport because mine didn't have a certain wording on the first page. The wording was on the third page, but the civil servant wouldn't accept this.

When I applied for Spanish nationality after ten years' residence and ten years' marriage to a Spaniard, the paperwork was a nightmare and I had to prove that I had lived in Spain before my marriage, in spite of the fact that being married to a Spaniard automatically qualifies the spouse for citizenship! Eventually I was awarded citizenship on residence grounds, even though my husband and two daughters were Spanish. The final step involved an interview at the police station, where questions included whether I liked Spain or not and what I thought of the Gibraltar situation! I obviously gave the right answers because I was awarded citizenship.

As an aside, on the subject of Gibraltar, I don't think that the average Spanish person is as interested in its future as some Spanish politicians like to suggest – the type of politician who wants to generate publicity by talking about controversial subjects. It is, however, a contentious issue for Spaniards living near the border, especially in La Linea and Algeciras. They are indignant about the smuggling that goes on in Gibraltar, particularly of cigarettes, and also about the money laundering, and they object to the oil spillages taking place there and the presence of British and other nuclear submarines. The arrival of the nuclear submarine 'Tireless' was a particular concern, as was the appearance of a single-hulled oil tanker shortly after the disastrous 'Prestige' spillage in Galicia, which was a serious worry for people all along this coast.

Returning to red tape, I have received maternity benefit on two occasions, sick pay for a month and unemployment benefit on two occasions. All payments were received in arrears to start with and there was rather a lot of paperwork to get the payments, but otherwise the system worked quite well. The major downside is the queues everywhere.

Social security contributions are very high for self-employed people and I am tired of receiving costly, glossy leaflets from the Ministry of Employment telling me about everything they are doing for us, but failing to inform us of when the monthly payments go up. I also think we get relatively few benefits for such high payments, but that is probably the same all over the world.

As for taxes, I have inevitably made numerous tax declarations in my time, but all of them have been in my favour! And I am always amazed that when the authorities write to you to tell you that you have made a mistake and they actually owe you money, they give you the option to appeal against this or renounce the refund! But they take far too long to refund money, despite their publicity claiming that most people get it back in a couple of months. Five months is the shortest period I have had to wait.

Spanish Schools

Spanish schools are usually pretty good. The education system is very much based on learning by rote and teaching revolves around the textbook. Children are given an excellent grounding in basics and their general knowledge of just about everything is also excellent. But in the state system, the teachers are very much civil servants and don't usually work additional hours or do anything extra for their pupils, unless they are unusually dedicated teachers.

Even though I am English, my children are strongly Spanish, and it must be said that the Spanish are beginning to become indignant about the number of foreign children in the state schools, particularly in the schools with most foreigners, which are on the Costa del Sol and Costa Blanca. The main problem is that with children of so many nationalities and differing Spanish language skills, the teachers often have to repeat everything, usually several times, before all the children in the class grasp it. And this obviously slows the education process for everybody, so the foreigners are seen to be holding back the local children.

My daughters are scathing about their peers who don't speak Spanish because it wastes so much of their time. They were especially unimpressed by one British boy who, despite having been in Spain for four years, still speaks only basic Spanish. And yet there is an Estonian pupil who is approaching fluency, despite having been here for only nine months. Part of the problem, it seems, is the lack of interest in Spanish shown by too many British parents at home.

It is partly a matter of finance, I think. Better-off Brits tend to send their kids to fee-paying international schools, which teach them Spanish or perhaps pay for a tutor. But for quite a lot of foreign kids in Spanish state schools – particularly language-resistant British children – there is a strong possibility of there being a generation of them who are only half literate in two languages: their written English will be basic because they are learning it at a Spanish school, while their spoken Spanish will be poor because they don't speak it at home.

The attitude of some British parents amazes and appals me. One couple I know of expressed their great disappointment to discover that the teachers at the Spanish state school their child attends didn't all speak English! With parents whose attitude is so far removed from reality, what chance does the poor kid have?

Friends & Frustrations

People have a mixed experience of making friends in Spain. Where we live now, we haven't made any close friends among our neighbours, not because they aren't nice people but because they tend to be here for brief visits or are much older than us, often retired. But we have made friends from many different countries, which I find very interesting – and definitely one of the advantages of living in a cosmopolitan region like this.

Looking back to my time in Granada, I remember that many of my British friends seemed to be running away from something in the UK, like a divorce, failed job, bereavement or whatever. But I don't think that is uncommon with expatriates everywhere, and not just British ones.

> *Spaniards are very friendly and welcoming on a superficial level, but it is quite difficult to become close friends with them*

I think Spaniards can be difficult to get to know well. They are very friendly and welcoming on a superficial level, but it is quite difficult to break through further and become close friends with them. It is partly because the Spanish are still very family-oriented and many of their friends come from the extended family. And because many Spaniards still aren't very mobile, family and school friends live close together for their whole lives and people don't see the need to make new friends. Brits and other foreigners seem to move around more and are used to making friends where they move to.

Many Spaniards on the coast are frustrated and puzzled by the general British refusal to learn Spanish. We definitely stand out from the hoard of foreigners in our unwillingness to integrate, particularly in learning the language. My husband is always offended that our immediate neighbours greet him in English rather than in Spanish. Needless to say, he always replies in Spanish! Many Spaniards are also amazed at how little foreigners adapt to the Spanish timetable and expect to go shopping or a workman to come round at 3pm, for example. And some of our behaviour offends the Spanish – even seemingly unimportant things like not wearing shirts around town. Perhaps it's a hangover from Catholic Puritanism.

I think we have a very high quality of life here – better than in Britain. It is generally safe, the climate is lovely, there is a relaxed outlook on life and little evidence of class division. I also like the emphasis on family in Spain and the fact that Spaniards love children and have all the time in the world for them. And I enjoy the food, culture and gorgeous natural surroundings. We also enjoy visiting other parts of Spain and are considering a move to Catalonia when the girls leave home – it's an area we love.

The gripes we have about living here include the poor postal service, the fact that some places have become too built-up, and the heat and crowds in July and

August. And I also sometimes worry about the competence of the local authorities and the massive debts they run up; Marbella is an example of that.

if you accept that a foreign
country is going to be different,
you will adapt much more easily

I suppose we could also do with better public transport and we sometimes despair at the buck-passing that goes on between the local, provincial and national tiers of government.

If you are considering a move to Spain, do a lot of homework about all aspects of living here before you come out and make learning Spanish your number one priority and stick to it. Don't expect things to be as they are in your home country and don't complain if they aren't. If you accept that a foreign country is going to be different, you will adapt much more easily.

Season Ticket

Tony Hughes swapped biochemistry in Manchester
for retail management in Fuengirola, via a stint of
medical research in Barcelona, but three years
later, despite having a degree in Spanish,
he still feels in transition.

My first involvement with Spain was at school, when I began to learn the language at around twelve years of age. To be honest, I decided to study Spanish for little reason other than because I liked the teacher! But it turned out to be a good move in view of the way my life has developed. When you look at the general question of language teaching in Britain, I can't really understand why British schools continue to teach French as the compulsory foreign language because, globally, there are far more Spanish speakers than French speakers. According to the British Council, which isn't known for making extravagant claims, the number of French speakers (as a mother tongue and good-standard, second language) is 125 million, but the number of Spanish speakers (using the same criteria) is 450 million. Joint top are English and Mandarin Chinese, with around a billion each.

So I was steeped in Spain and its culture from quite an early age, although sometimes inaccurately: very few Spaniards dance flamenco and eat paella three times a day, although to judge by some of the lessons we had, you would think they did! I took Spanish GCSE and A Level, among others, and then did a degree at Manchester University in biochemistry and Spanish, although, despite this strong background in Spanish, the decision to come to Spain was actually more down to fate than choice.

I graduated with a 2:2 grade degree, which isn't quite good enough to pursue a worthwhile career in my main subject, biochemistry. I was really gutted at the time and didn't have a clue what to do with my life. Eventually, I decided either to dedicate my career to retail management (which I had been doing as a part-time job while studying in Manchester) or try to do something which involved Spanish, as it seemed a shame not to continue with the language after several years of study.

Whether down to luck, fate or whatever you want to call it, I was able to do both. The following week, an internal memo at my place of part-time work advertised positions as retail managers in Spain. Hey presto – a timely opportunity which was too good to miss. As for why I decided to come to Malaga province, that was an easy one: the company only operated here so the decision was made for me. And so in 2001, I headed off to sunny Fuengirola and, at the grand old age of 26, I am still here.

Castilian & Catalan

My degree was a four-year course, which involved spending most of the third year abroad. I chose to go to Barcelona and, although people might think that was because I am a culture-vulture, fan of architecture and food lover, to be honest, it was more for the football than any other reason!

I spent nine months in the city, working in cancer research by day, and enjoying all that the city has to offer by night. Looking back on that work as a researcher, while it was interesting, it probably showed me that I am not actually cut out for biochemical research. That is because it can be very negative, in the sense that most things don't work as new treatments or help to advance existing ones, although that of course is a sort of progress – ruling things out. But hindsight has shown me that a career in biochemistry possibly isn't for me. And I can thank my first period in Spain for that.

> **" I would advise anybody learning a foreign language to try to take a course that emphasises speaking rather than writing "**

I had a strange experience with the language when I arrived in Barcelona. Despite having studied Spanish since the age of twelve and being pretty competent, it took me at least a month before I felt comfortable speaking it after I arrived in Barcelona. And not only did I speak good Castilian Spanish, I had also done some Catalan in my second year to prepare for my time in Barcelona. As to why I was uncomfortable speaking the languages, I put it down to the British language-teaching stress on writing rather than speaking. I would advise anybody learning a foreign language to try to take a course that stresses speaking rather than writing.

It probably didn't help me that the research in Barcelona was all undertaken in English, even though most of the researchers were Spanish, so I missed out on daily language practice at work. Everybody spoke English because much of the global research and resources in the field come from America, which of course is an English-speaking country. Most of my fellow workers spoke English with an American accent, having spent a year or so training in the US.

Living in Barcelona was rather different from living on the Costa del Sol. I think I found it easier to settle in Barcelona. Like a lot of cities, it is full of people from elsewhere, and the fact that even many of the Spaniards were 'strangers' made it easier to settle in and integrate. That said, you not only have to contend with speaking Spanish, but you must also remember that the locals invariably speak Catalan by preference. They are more tolerant of foreigners speaking Castilian, but if you really want to integrate, you need to learn Catalan. In fact, so proud are many of the locals of their Catalan culture and language that they are happier speaking to you in English than Castilian Spanish!

Don't imagine that Castilian and Catalan are similar. They might look it on paper, but the pronunciations are very different. That is best shown by the fact that when somebody is speaking Catalan on Spanish TV, it is subtitled into Castilian at the bottom of the screen. And it isn't just the language that is different: the Catalans see themselves as separate from the rest of Spain. They are sometimes characterised as the most hard-working, outward-looking and creative of Spaniards, and they are definitely more business and efficiency-oriented than people in Andalusia. They are like a cross between Latins and North Europeans, with the flair of the former and the work ethic of the latter. It's an attractive combination.

The British In Barcelona

The people in Barcelona, and Catalonia as a whole, are open-minded, friendly and international looking, so they welcome foreigners. However, there is a certain degree of anti-Britishness in the region, stemming, I think, from our empire. The reasoning behind this is that the British, like the Catalans' 'enemies' the Spanish, imposed their will on others, so they view us negatively, as they do the Spanish. In fact, I came across a surprising number of locals who really liked the film 'Braveheart', because it showed the English getting their bums kicked!

if you are used to big-city facilities, attractions and culture, seaside towns and rural areas can be pretty dull

There is also a perception among some people in Barcelona that the British, particularly the English (although people don't always understand the distinction), are hooligans. Unfortunately, this is true in many European countries, but perhaps particularly so in football-mad places like Barcelona, which have had to put up with visiting English football supporters. The local definition of a hooligan, by the way, isn't just a shaven-headed, tattooed yob who fights with opposition football fans; he is anybody who walks around town with his shirt off and spends much of his time drinking pints of beer in public. Barcelona is a particularly chic, stylish city, with trendy, sophisticated people, and that kind of behaviour is very much looked down upon. You have been warned.

Nevertheless, Barcelona is a wonderful place for a foreigner to live. Although it is a large, stylish, cultivated place, it is usually inexpensive, and the range of cultural, artistic and sporting activities open to you is vast. It is also a good staging post for visiting the rest of mainland Spain, the Balearics, southern France and even northern Italy, which isn't too much of a drive.

I think that a fair few Brits who have previously lived in British cities and who want to emigrate here should try a Spanish city before heading for the Costas or islands. If you are used to big-city facilities, attractions and culture, seaside towns and rural areas can be pretty dull and one-dimensional. I don't just mean Spanish ones, but seaside and country towns the world over.

Language Lessons

I didn't find the transition difficult when I moved to Spain, partly because I had lived in the country before and also because I spoke the language. For both reasons, I am not a typical Brit in this country. Despite this, I still gave myself time to adjust and acclimatise – between four and six weeks. During that period, you must try to keep an open mind and absorb as much as you can about your new environment. Watch out for what the locals do and when, bar opening hours and the other minutiae of everyday life: when in Rome, do as the Romans do, as the cliché tells us. Having said that, I am not sure that the transitional period ever really ends, and even now things occur on most days that might be described as culture shock. Don't be under the illusion that Spain is like Britain with sunshine: the lifestyle and mindset are really pretty different.

I think that my ability with the Spanish language has improved because of my work, in a retail department. Although plenty of our customers are English-speakers, all the other staff are Spanish, so I get practice every day talking to them. It is one of those situations where you are forced to speak Spanish, which is possibly the best way for us language-shy Brits to learn. I would also recommend that people watch television because it is a great way to increase your vocabulary, although you will quickly find out that 'real' people don't tend to speak as slowly and clearly as a lot of the people on television. It is the same elsewhere of course: how many Brits, for example, speak BBC English?

I think that people should also try to have fun learning the language. It is sometimes hard to avoid it. For example, the Spanish for cushions is *cojines*, while the word for testicles is *cojones*, which can cause problems when you are working in the home interiors department. I once asked a work colleague to get out his testicles and put them on a shelf. The look on his face was priceless!

Despite such 'misunderstandings', I think the fact that I can speak Spanish and try to follow Spanish customs has earned me the respect of my colleagues and increased my work prospects immeasurably. If you can achieve the same, your social and work prospects will broaden greatly. In fact, I think the piece of advice people will read most often in this book is 'learn the language'. You can certainly survive here without speaking any Spanish, but you will severely restrict yourself.

The strong Andalusian accent is sometimes used as an excuse by foreigners for not learning the language and it is true that it's rather thick. People tend to chew their words and they often only pronounce half of them. For example, *hasta luego* (see you later) becomes, *a uego*, delivered in a guttural grunt. But think about

British accents and what foreign English-speakers have to contend with: Scouse, Geordie, Cockney, Glaswegian, Brum and all the rest.

Bothersome Bureaucracy

I haven't been exposed to too much bureaucracy and red tape because I don't run my own business, I haven't bought a property here and I don't have any children, so I have avoided anything to do with estate agents, lawyers and schools. Having said that, I found getting an *NIE* number difficult because at the police station they wanted proof of employment, i.e. a contract, prior to processing the request. However, I couldn't obtain an official contract, because in order to get one you need – wait for it – an *NIE* number! We got around the problem by my employers sending an explanatory letter to the police.

This type of bureaucratic inefficiency and frustration is quite common in Spain and is probably explained by the fact that the country employs so many people in local government, all trying to justify their jobs by over-complicating everything: I read that it's something ridiculous like ten per cent of the workforce. I get the impression that things are better than they used to be – partly because of the introduction of computers – but if you move to Spain you will still have to try to get used to quite a lot of foot-dragging inefficiency.

When I applied for residence, I was amazed at how long the process took: five months. And in order to see it through, you have to do a lot of queuing and call on all your reserves of patience. My application might have taken longer than average because I applied at the height of the tourist season, when a lot of other people were doing so too and some of the officials were probably away on holiday themselves. There is also the fact that I live in a major tourist area, Fuengirola, which has a higher than average number of applications to process.

But not everything is badly run in Spain. Contrary to expectation, I have found banking a breeze. I bank with a Spanish-operated branch of a well known German bank: opening the account was a doddle and there are never any queues, although I am not sure that is the case with some of the Spanish-owned banks. Shop around, because some banks are better and more efficient than others. And I would recommend that people avoid using bankers' drafts or cheques to transfer money from foreign accounts to Spanish accounts. It took an amazing six weeks from the time I put money into my account to the time I was able to access it.

As for using the health service, as long as you have a social security card, there is nothing else to worry about. I have only seen the doctor once – with a minor sprain of the hand. I waited about an hour and a half in Accident and Emergency, and was dealt with very professionally. As an aside to this – and sorry to keep going on about language – but if you don't speak Spanish you might have problems, because a lot of Spanish doctors and nurses speak little if any English. Some of the medical centres have volunteer translators to help foreigners, but some don't. And at the centres which do have them, they are much in demand and you might have to wait a long time for one to be free.

Making Connections

The British friends I have tend to be around ten years older than me, probably because I am rather younger than the average expat. But I find that too many of the Brits here are wannabe wideboys and not really the type of people I want to be friends with. And perhaps it is more difficult to make friends as a single person, rather than as part of a couple, although I think that is the case everywhere, not just in Spain.

As for making Spanish friends, I found it easier in Barcelona and also in Vélez-Málaga (a largish town inland of the eastern Costa del Sol), where I lived for a while. I have already explained why it was easier in Barcelona, and in Vélez I think it was because I shared a flat with a Spanish girl and I used to go out with her and her friends. Part of the difficulty in connecting with Spanish people in Fuengirola is that they are rather regimented in their lives and only socialise on a Friday and Saturday. A lot of them wouldn't dream of going out on, say, a Tuesday, because it just isn't done.

so bad are some people's manners that I sometimes find myself apologising to my Spanish colleagues for being British

The town also has a traditional attitude, whereby people hook up with their friends and girlfriend/boyfriend at school and then stick with them, perhaps not seeing the need for other friends. But this small town attitude isn't unique to Andalusia or Spain; I think it is found throughout the world. However, it is a surprise that in a town with so many foreign holidaymakers and permanent residents there aren't more clubs and organisations promoting cross-cultural contacts and friendships. We all seem to stick to our own.

One local exception to this is Malaga Football Club, which is enthusiastically supported by a lot of foreigners all along the Costa del Sol; they get bussed in from quite a long way away. I think around ten per cent of the club's season ticket holders are foreign, the majority of them British. So that is a point of connection between the locals and the foreigners, although quite a lot of local Spaniards, like people in many parts of the country, support one of the country's big two teams, Real Madrid and Barcelona, which is wrong of course! You should follow the team nearest to where you were born – it's actually an arbitrary accident of geography as to who you support.

I can sympathise with those Spaniards who have a problem with the foreigners living here, particularly those who won't speak Spanish or make any attempt to integrate. You would be amazed at the number of foreigners – mainly Brits – who waltz into our shop and expect all the staff to speak English. In fact, they look surprised or even resentful if they don't. So bad are some people's manners that I sometimes find myself apologising to my Spanish colleagues for being British!

Although the Spanish are generally tolerant and welcoming, they tend to regard a lot of the foreigners as *guiris*, which can be defined as a North European tourist who, no matter what time of the year it is, wears shorts, a vest or T-shirt, and socks with flip-flops, who spends the day drinking beer on the seafront, and who lacks education, manners and culture. In fact, they lump us together and tend to call all North Europeans Brits, because we are the most numerous group around here. Of course it is an exaggeration to claim that all Brits conform to this *guiri* stereotype, but in Fuengirola we definitely get more than our fair share of people who don't know how to dress or behave properly.

Overall, my quality of life is better here than it was in Britain. I feel more relaxed, I am not tied to my watch as much as I was in England and I feel safer. I tend to like Spanish people, which really helps, and find my biggest dislike is the type of foreigner who the Spanish call a *guiri*.

> *try to be like a sponge,*
> *absorbing as much as you can.*
> *You also have to be proactive,*
> *and get yourself out there,*
> *especially if you're single*

I can indulge my passion for football and am a season ticket holder at Malaga CF. At home, as well as tickets being a lot more expensive, I couldn't even get on the list for a season ticket to Manchester City. I have also begun to jog regularly, something I never did in England; the weather is more conducive to it in Spain. And the local social life doesn't just revolve around drinking, as it tended to back in the UK. I suppose that the acid test is to ask whether I would do it again, and the answer is a definite yes. I certainly don't rule out a return to England at some stage, but not now because I feel at home here.

I would recommend that people thinking of coming to Spain go for it, but move here only if you intend to try to integrate with the locals, immersing yourself in their language and culture. Otherwise, living in Fuengirola or a town like it would resemble living in Blackpool in the sun, which might be okay for a while, but not for too long. But I would also advise people to be patient. It will take rather longer to integrate than you think – as do many things in Spain – so you will have to stick with it. Try to be like a sponge, absorbing as much as you can. You also have to be proactive, and get yourself out there, especially if you're single.

Costa Del Concrete

Scot Adam Shreeve moved with his English wife, Anne, from London to Estepona to escape the rat race and do something he liked doing, but the attractions of the Costa del Sol soon wore off.

I began to think about a major life-change when I reached the age of thirty and had a sort of minor life crisis, or 'menopause'. There wasn't anything very original about it: just the usual stuff about where am I going, what am I doing, am I happy, and do I want to be living my life like this in a decade? I realised that I needed to change radically. Despite having a good job, quite a lot of money and a great place to live in a good part of London, I wasn't really happy. And the stress was beginning to take its toll.

I had always wanted to paint and realised that it was the ideal time; probably now or never. Anne was open to the idea of change, so we started to think about where to go to live the dream of a less stressful, more fulfilled life. We considered Cornwall and rural Scotland, but neither of us like the cold and rain, so ruled them out. And we also thought that we should probably have a go at living abroad, so we began to contemplate Spain. We had been there on holiday a couple of times, staying at Anne's parents' place in Estepona on the Costa del Sol, so it seemed the obvious and easy option.

Despite its sometimes dodgy image as a nightmare concrete jungle in a heatwave, a decade ago the Costa del Sol was less developed than it is now, less crowded and much cheaper, and seemed the ideal place to make a downsizing career switch. The decision to move to Estepona was arbitrary, decided simply by the fact that Anne's mum and dad had an apartment there that we could stay in while we found our feet, rather than because of a particular love of the town. But it is a nice place, one of the better spots on the Costa del Sol.

A Large Undertaking

We found the transition to life in Spain pretty smooth, but I think we did it sensibly and made it as easy as possible for ourselves. Once we had decided to go, it was eighteen months before we actually made the break from Britain because there was a lot to arrange. In the interim, we did up both our properties in UK, one to sell, the other to rent out. We also took Spanish classes, which meant that by the time we arrived in Spain we were at a decent standard – maybe O Level.

 emigrating is a large undertaking: think moving house and then treble it, maybe more

The eighteen months between deciding to go and actually going also gave our families and friends time to adjust to the idea, which came out of the blue for most of them. I think the fact that your nearest and dearest are also affected by your decision to emigrate is something that too many people overlook.

When we finally arrived in Spain, we took a couple of months off and treated them as an extended holiday more than a settling-in period. We really needed the break. Emigrating is a large undertaking: think moving house and then treble it, maybe more. So we really eased ourselves in gently. As well as that, we were living in a flat we knew, in a town we knew, and were surrounded by plenty of English-speaking expats on the urbanisation, many of whom we knew through Anne's parents. Added to that, we didn't need to worry too much about working straight away because we had put aside a fair amount of money to pay for the settling-in period. And we didn't have children – still don't – so didn't have to think about schooling, etc.

We moved out in August and waited until October before really beginning our life in Spain. That made it much easier, because the heat and crowds of the main season had receded by then. And we integrated into the local community quite easily, although that didn't involve many Spanish people, because most of our neighbours and the people we came across were British, Danish, Swedish, German and Finnish. The part of the coast we were living on could better be described as an international zone rather than a part of Spain. And the most commonly spoken language was English.

As for mixing with the locals, being able to speak better Spanish than the average Brit helped, and the fact that we were much younger than many expats also meant that we stood out. But we didn't become close to any Spanish people for a number of years. It sounds ridiculous when I say that, but it just happened, as it does with so many foreigners here.

As for the lifestyle, we really enjoyed it. Ten years ago, the Costa del Sol was rather less built-up than it is now and much less expensive. It was ideal to begin a new career, while being able to have a reasonable lifestyle for not too much money. And because we still had a property in England, we hadn't burned all our bridges and knew that we could go back if things didn't go well in Spain; that was good to know and I would recommend that other people do the same, if possible. It isn't as easy to manage now as it was then, however, because property prices and rents on the Costa have risen so much over the past decade.

The first thing to say about learning Spanish is, 'Don't expect it to be easy'. There seems to be a general perception that Spanish is a straightforward language to learn, but I don't think it is easy to learn properly. I would agree that you can probably learn to speak basic Spanish more quickly than you can some other languages – German, for example – but it is hard to learn to speak it well. And if you want to integrate properly, you will need to speak it properly.

When starting, I would recommend that you get a tutor rather than go to classes. It is obviously more expensive per pupil to have somebody teach a small group rather than a class, but you learn much more and more quickly. You have to: when there is only a handful of you, there is nowhere to hide from teacher! I know people who have been to Spanish classes for years, but they haven't learned much because there are twenty-five or thirty pupils in the class, often from several different countries, and you are always held back by the slowest pupil.

After you have learned the basics, try to use your Spanish as often as possible. That means talking to people in the queue at the butcher, to taxi drivers, to the guy who cuts your grass, to everybody who is unlucky enough to cross your path. Try to find a conversation buddy, i.e. a native Spanish speaker whose English is roughly at the same level as your Spanish. Try to meet them at least a couple of times a week for an hour or so each time, and spend half the session speaking Spanish, the other half English. As well as this being the best way to improve your conversational Spanish, you might also make friends.

Plenty of Spaniards want and/or need to learn English, it being the *lingua franca* in many Spanish tourist regions, so you shouldn't have too much trouble finding people. Finding people who will actually turn up regularly, however, is another matter. And the Andalusian accent is famously strong so you will have to adjust your ear, and when you start it might be easier if you can find a conversation buddy from Valladolid, Salamanca, Madrid or another place where they speak pure, clear Spanish. I have also found that Mexicans and Argentineans speak 'nice' Spanish. Best of all, apparently, is to find a Spanish-speaking girlfriend or boyfriend. Pillow talk is allegedly the best way to learn a new language, but I can't talk from personal experience.

A Large Retirement Home

I don't think we even began to integrate into Spanish society while we lived on the Costa. It wasn't through a lack of desire, so much as circumstances. Anne, who always found the language rather more difficult than me, got a job with an English firm dealing almost exclusively with British clients, while I worked from home on my own, so didn't come into contact with many locals either.

I also think that the locals weren't particularly interested in befriending foreigners. To be frank, looking at some of us, I don't blame them! But it seems to me that a lot of Spanish people are as much family- as friend-oriented, unlike in Britain, where it is said that friends are the new family. (I can understand why, because you can choose your friends, but not your family). The Spanish also tend to go out and about in large groups of family and/or friends, rather than in smaller ones as we do. There is a group rather than individual friendship mentality here and it can be difficult to penetrate the group.

As for the Spanish way of life and *modus operandi*, some aspects are great, others are very frustrating, and I haven't really got used to the latter. I like their attitude of work to live rather than the City of London idea of live to work. The siesta is one of the world's great inventions, as are tapas, and bars and restaurants staying open until all hours, which make for a more flexible social life. But the *mañana* attitude can be very wearing if you are trying to get something done, whether it is something supposedly very simple like having a gas bottle delivered, or a big thing like buying a business. Things take a lot longer than they need to and are quite often botched. People don't always seem to take a lot of pride in their work here. And the obvious inefficiency and corruption of local government adversely affects many aspects of life.

> *some days I used to wander around our town on the Costa del Sol and feel like I was the only person under sixty*

I think foreigners on the Costas sometimes find it hard to make friends; or rather, hard to keep them. A lot of people are transient, coming down for a year or two and then moving on. Two of my closer friends, both English, returned to the UK in the year before we relocated to Minorca. I am not saying that this doesn't happen elsewhere, but it is more common on the Costas and in other holiday regions, not just Spanish ones.

Younger expats still find that most other foreigners here are over fifty, so you will have a limited pool of foreigners of similar age to make friends with. There are more younger people coming out now than there were when we arrived ten years ago, but a lot don't stay for more than a couple of years. And in the months between October and Easter, many coastal and island towns in Spain take on the feeling of large retirement homes. So many sun-starved north European retirees come out to Spain for several weeks or months to escape the northern winter that younger people sometimes feel a bit swamped by them. Some days I used to wander around our town on the Costa del Sol and feel like I was the only person under sixty. And so many bars and restaurants offer bingo, music hall-type acts, dances, quizzes and other things to attract senior citizens. I am reminded of Ruby Wax's comment that Miami was full of old people 'sitting around the pool waiting for lunch or death, whichever came first'.

There is also the class/cultural aspect to friendships in Spain; we Brits don't seem able to escape the class thing, do we? If you want to live with people of a similar background to you on the Costa del Sol, you will need to pick your town carefully: the Marbella area definitely attracts a more upmarket type of Brit, as do the areas around Estepona, Mijas and Nerja. But a lot of the coastal developments seem to be filled with unreconstructed working-class geezers and wannabe geezers, working in timeshare, real estate and other potentially dodgy fields.

That is a generalisation, of course, but these geezer types are very visible and part of the reason that Brits abroad have such a bad reputation. So there is a limited younger British expat pool to make friends from, which is further severely reduced if you are a nice middle-class bloke like me, who sometimes wants to talk about arty and academic matters. That is one of the reasons we moved to Minorca: you get more people like me here. It also has to be said that the Costa is generally a cultural desert. But that is the case with holiday regions the world over. Apart from sea, sand, sangria and thousands of bars and restaurants, there isn't much.

> *being seen to be drunk in public is quite a no-no in Spain and our close relationship with booze makes us look bad in their eyes*

One of the social successes of our time on the Costa del Sol, however, was meeting Danes, many of whom live there. Anne and I usually like and get on well with Danish people and we have made a couple of close Danish friends, who we will definitely stay in touch with. They have a relish for life, are open-minded and invariably speak excellent English, as well as better Spanish than we Brits.

I did like the international aspect of life on the Costa del Sol. You meet people from all over the world and they generally rub along quite well together, although the Muslim and Chinese communities seem to be isolated from the rest, but that isn't peculiar to Spain unfortunately.

Moving To Minorca

I think that the Spanish are generally tolerant and guardedly welcoming. They are pragmatic, realising that the region has benefited from foreigners a lot more than it has suffered from them, and there are still plenty who remember how poor and undeveloped the Costa del Sol was before the foreign money began to arrive thirty or forty years ago. That said, I think a lot of them wonder why we have come to their country when all we seem to want to do is to recreate our home country as much as possible, with the addition of sunshine. And they are frustrated by our inability and unwillingness to learn their language.

I know some Spanish people who have a very mixed idea of foreigners, the British in particular. At our best, they really like us and admire our history, business success, music, culture and style, but they also see the yob element. An Anglophile Spanish friend once perceptively said to me that the British are a nation of extremes: the very good and the bloody awful. He thinks the same about North Americans.

Spanish people also object to us coming here and complaining about bullfighting and the way donkeys and other animals are treated when we have fox hunting. There isn't much you can say to that really. On a completely different tack, I know some Spaniards who take a dim view of the way that some north European girls and women dress, or rather underdress, and behave, or misbehave. And they cannot understand why we feel the need to drink so much alcohol. Being seen to be drunk in public is quite a no-no in Spain and our close relationship with booze makes us look bad in their eyes.

Interestingly, I think that the arrival of David Beckham in Spain might have changed the image of Brits. He is seen as a hard-working, stylish, abstemious family man, and that has maybe helped our image a bit. Am I grasping at straws? Perhaps, because I also know people who are appalled at the tattoo he has had made on the back of his neck, which is visible all the time. I wonder why the British are so fond of tattoos?

When we visited the island of Minorca on holiday, we really noticed the contrast with the Costa del Sol. Minorca is still quite underdeveloped, green and tranquil, and it attracts a different type of holidaymaker and foreign resident: quieter and more arty, as well as the bird watchers who come to observe the feathered creatures that visit the island during their migrations; they seem to be a pleasant if strangely obsessional bunch. And there seem to be fewer dodgy people and 'wide boys' here, whereas the Costa del Sol is quite badly polluted by them.

We felt comfortable here immediately and relished the chance to live somewhere quiet, isolated even. I wouldn't recommend it for people who like a lively social life. Out of season – October to Easter – the island half shuts and you have to make your own amusement. And the weather isn't nearly as good in the winter as it is on the Costa del Sol. I prefer it here in the summer though, because it is cooler and breezier, but the winter weather can be very wet and windy, for long periods. And it can be pretty cold too.

We are actually thinking about moving to Majorca some time. It is much bigger than Minorca and more developed, but there are also plenty of quieter areas too, so you can have the best of both worlds. And there are a lot more flights to and from the UK, where we like to return regularly, and more tourists too, who will hopefully buy my pictures!

We were also attracted to the Balearics because the local authorities seem to have a more sensible attitude to development than they do on the Costas. Majorca in particular is trying to right some of the carbuncles built on the island in the 1960s and '70s, and trying to manage future development. It is difficult to balance development and ecology, but at least they have recognised the problem and are trying to do something. There was also a short-lived 'eco tax', paid by visitors to help with protecting the island's ecology but it was unpopular and voted out.

Life on islands can be more expensive than on the mainland because more things have to be shipped in. And after living in the large country of Spain, I can understand if people might feel claustrophobic on little Minorca. We don't, but I know of people who do.

Living & Working In Spain

It can be difficult for foreigners to find work in Spain if they don't have specific skills or qualifications – whether as a doctor, plumber, artist or whatever – or who aren't flexible self-starters. Anne and I have been okay because I have the painting and sculpture (which sell steadily rather than remarkably) and she works from her computer. But we know of a lot of people who have struggled.

I don't think the employment situation is unique to Spain, but to holiday areas the world over. A lot of the work that is available is in the tourist trade – hotels, restaurants, bars, car hire and the rest – and these are traditionally badly paid and require you to work long, unsocial hours, often every day of the week during the high season. That takes its toll on people, and they get little financial reward. And they don't get the time to enjoy the relaxed, sunny life in Spain.

There also doesn't seem to be much job security and a lot of people work without proper employment contracts, who therefore have no rights to unemployment pay, healthcare, etc. The trouble is that in desirable places to live, employers know that the supply of labour exceeds the number of jobs, so they don't need to pay well or give contracts in order to attract employees. So quite a lot of Brits, particularly on the Costa del Sol, live from hand to mouth, pottering between jobs. That might be okay in your later teens and twenties, and at a push your thirties, but older people are looking for more security. And I am not sure that Spain is the best place to come for that.

I think that unhappiness with pay and working conditions is one of the main reasons for people returning to the UK, usually after a couple of years. And I think it will get worse for Western Europeans following the expansion of the EU: more East Europeans are coming to Spain, prepared to work for low wages.

The first thing I would say to anybody thinking of coming to Spain – and this actually applies to a move to any foreign country – is to ask yourself why you are moving. If you have an enthusiasm for Spain, France, Australia or wherever, fine, but if you are only moving because you are unhappy with your life in Britain or wherever, it might not work. In fact, the move abroad might make things worse. If, for example, you are working in the wrong job, in the wrong relationship or whatever in the UK, simply transplanting the problem to another country won't necessarily help. In fact, the undoubted pressures of emigration might make things worse.

The second recommendation is not to cut off all ties with the home country. It is tempting, especially if you are in a 'the grass is greener over the fence' frame of mind, but you might find yourself missing Britain and wanting to return. A lot of people do. I know that I have lived away from it for a decade but, having travelled quite extensively, I would still say that the UK is one of the very best places in the world in which to live. You might only realise that after you have left it.

*you miss out on a great deal
if you don't speak at least
some Spanish . . . if you make
the effort, you can generate a
lot of goodwill with the locals*

Third, rent before you buy. And try to rent in the area of Spain you are intending to live in for at least a year before deciding to buy. You need to see it throughout the year, in good weather and bad, and when there are plenty and few tourists, to decide whether it is for you. Don't be afraid to change your mind and move elsewhere. In fact, the chances of getting it right first, second or even third time are quite low.

Fourth, learn the language. You can live your life on the Costa del Sol and the islands without a word of Spanish – and a lot of foreigners do – with English-language newspapers, magazines, radio and television stations and English-speaking bar and restaurant owners, plumbers, lawyers, estate agents, the lot, but you miss out on a great deal if you don't speak at least some Spanish. I am not sure how many Brits ever become fluent – it is difficult, learning as an adult, to become so in a foreign tongue – but more of us should try and be seen to be trying. If you make the effort, however incompetent the results, you can generate a lot of goodwill with the locals.

Fifth, try living in coastal, rural and urban environments, to see which suits you best. A lot of people automatically head for the coast, but there are lovely places to live inland and in the cities. I am a great fan of Malaga, Madrid, Palma and Barcelona. Try them.

Life In A Warm Climate

Karen McMahon abandoned a successful marketing career in Britain to sell timeshare on the Costa del Sol. It wasn't only her friends and family who thought she had gone mad.

It is really my parents' fault that I'm here. They bought a holiday home back in 1982 in La Carihuela (between Torrelmolinos and Malaga, on the Costa del Sol) and subsequently sold that and bought a series of properties in nearby Benalmadena. They now have a place in Churriana, which is a town inland of Malaga. I had been holidaying in their properties in Spain for over a decade before I came to live here. In fact, I used to come out four or five times a year, sometimes just for long weekends, so I got to know the area really well. And I would recommend that other people do likewise before considering living here.

I decided as early as the mid-1980s that I would come to Spain eventually to live, but it took me another decade to get here. The main reason I wanted to come was that I have never liked the cold weather in Britain and wanted to live in a warm climate. I was going to come earlier on a couple of occasions, but I kept getting decent jobs in Britain. I am originally from Yorkshire and worked in marketing at the Crucible Theatre in Sheffield after I graduated (in English and Drama from Birmingham University), and then spent three years (1986 to 1989) in marketing for Nottingham County Council Leisure Services. After that, I did a similar job for the York Archaeological Trust, which involved looking after the Viking Centre and the Festival, writing for the Trust's magazine and other duties. That was from November 1989 to February 1994.

I then received two good job offers in the UK, but I had also heard of an opportunity in Spain, working in timeshare for Club la Costa, because my parents knew one of the senior people there. It was in-house selling, which was really a sort of extension of all the marketing work I had done in England. I had to think about it for a while because it was a commission-only job, but I slept on the decision, putting all negative thoughts from my mind, accepted the offer and moved out in March 1994.

A Head Start

Some of my family and friends thought I was crazy to do what I was doing. Not only was I turning down two good work offers in England, but I was taking a job in timeshare, which has never had a very good reputation or image. I think it was thoughts of the sunshine, late starts (but the finishes are late too!) and outdoor lifestyle in Spain that made the decision for me.

I found it easy to settle in, but as you can see from the above, I had been used to moving around and starting new jobs in different locations. I also had the two job offers back in the UK, and if it didn't work out here I knew that I would be able to return and find work quite easily. On top of that, I didn't burn all my bridges because I didn't sell my house in Britain. I rented it out and got a sound tenant, an army officer.

I think the fact that I had been out to Spain so often on holiday helped the transition, because I had a good idea of what living here would be like. And I hadn't only visited during the main summer season as so many people do. I had tended to come out in February, May and late October or November, so I had seen the coast at different times of the year, in good weather and bad. If you have only ever been here in the summer, the winter conditions can be quite a shock.

I also spoke quite good Spanish and that really helped. I had made the decision to come to live in Spain not long after I left university, so I had taken night classes in the language for two years and took an Institute of Linguistics exam, which I passed with distinction! That got me to O/A Level standard and I kept it up by using the language on my frequent holidays to Spain. So when I arrived permanently, I had a good base to build on, unlike so many Britons who come here knowing little or nothing of the language.

> *the Costa del Sol is much busier and more fast-paced than it was, and everybody seems greedier*

I have found it easy to make friends here, but I am used to moving around and meeting new people, and I am quite sociable anyway. Working for a large timeshare firm was also helpful, because it was a very buzzy, sociable environment, with lots of people of my age, from all over the place. In fact, a lot of the friends I made first were French and Spanish people working in timeshare, not other Brits, and I am still friends with some of them. To be frank, they were more sophisticated than many of the Britons, better educated and with more etiquette. I also found that talking to them was a good way to practise Spanish, although most also spoke English.

I think it was easier to make friends when I arrived here ten years ago than it is now. This area doesn't seem to be as laid-back and friendly as it was then. It is much busier and more fast-paced than it was, and everybody seems greedier. People sometimes say that it is difficult to make friends with the Spanish but I haven't found that. I have three Spanish friends who I think of as close friends. One is from Andalusia, one from Barcelona, and one from Madrid. I suppose you would describe all three as educated, with an open, international attitude. It is obviously easier as a foreigner to make friends with people like that than with closed-minded individuals.

But I am not sure that all Spanish people are that keen on the British, although having seen some real 'sights' down here, I sympathise. A Spanish nurse who was treating me recently thought I was Irish, perhaps because of my surname, and she really slagged off the English. She described us as stony-faced and rude, and didn't like the fact that so few of us bother to learn the language, or that we aren't family oriented enough for her liking. She liked the Irish more and thought them much more similar to the Spanish. Perhaps it is some type of Catholic solidarity. I kept my mouth shut about being English!

Racism & Sexism

Some Spanish people are racist – quite a few in fact. And they are quite vociferous and open about it. Maybe that will change and soften as the Spanish become more used to brown and black people – they are recent arrivals, for the most part – but for now it is becoming a problem. It seems to show that quite a few Spaniards have an instinctive dislike of outsiders and people who are different, so perhaps that explains why making friends with Spanish people can be difficult.

*there are also quite a lot of
men looking for rich women,
or even solvent women*

Spain is a very macho society, with some very old-fashioned attitudes towards women. You see it all the time, in your everyday life. If you overtake a man in your car, for example, and he notices that you are a woman, he doubles his efforts to overtake you back. And if you employ workmen to do anything, they find it hard to take orders or instructions from a woman, and they don't like their work being checked by a woman. They also invariably try to chat you up or ask you out.

On a broader level, I think it was more relaxed and easier for women here when I arrived ten years ago. It isn't as safe now and you have to be more careful. There are more and more dodgy characters around, from all sorts of countries. There are also quite a lot of men looking for rich women, or even solvent women. I have noticed a few times that, when I tell men what I do for a living, their interest picks up; I can almost see them thinking, "Hmm, she must do okay; I might be on to a cushy number here."

And there are definitely some men in their later thirties and early forties who are looking for well preserved ladies of fifty-plus who are well off because they have been widowed or got a good divorce settlement. I was amused and horrified to read of a recent scam – now broken up apparently – which preyed on the vanity of this sort of man. Adverts appeared in the classifieds section of some of the local papers asking for men interested in acting as escorts for ladies on the Costa del Sol. A number was given which you had to ring to supply further details, but it was a premium phone number and, when hopeful men rang up, they were kept on the line for ages giving their details and paying through the nose for the privilege of doing so, which is how the scam made its money. There was in fact no escort business and the men heard nothing more.

But maybe women are turning the tables on these men. I have just read about the arrest of six Spanish women who had also been swindling potential male escorts. They placed adverts guaranteeing men numerous potential lady customers on payment of between €300 and €500 (for customers in Spain only or worldwide) as a registration fee. No customers or meetings to discuss the business ever took place, but the clever women swindlers took it another step. The men were given a premium phone number to ring if they had any complaints, which of course all of them did. And when they rang the number, they were kept on the line for as long as possible and swindled twice! But I would advise women to be on the lookout for chancers and conmen. There are quite a lot down here.

Time In Timeshare

I found working in timeshare exciting, and you can earn a lot of money doing it. But like many sales jobs, it is almost totally commission-based, so if you don't sell, you don't earn anything. The pressure is relentless, there is little or no job security and staff turnover is very high. You are only as good as your last sale and, if you aren't selling well, they will get rid of you and employ somebody else. So I found it was easy to become jaded.

I found I had to take a holiday quite regularly because you become so tired that you begin to underperform and lose sales. In fact, you can tell you need a break when you begin to flag and miss sales that you know you would normally get. So you take time off to recharge your batteries. I usually found that my bosses didn't want me to take holidays but I had to explain why I was doing so and they usually relented. But everybody is under constant pressure at every level.

Working in the industry, you quickly discover that anything to do with timeshare has a really bad name. We even found that people who had bought our products were sometimes embarrassed or reluctant to tell their families and friends that they had bought a timeshare, so bad is its reputation, particularly among Britons and Germans. It doesn't seem to have so bad a name in the USA, at least for now. But if even some of the customers are embarrassed to be associated with the timeshare business, you can imagine what a bad reputation people who actually work in the industry have!

I think that a lot of other expatriates think timeshare people are the pits of the earth. It really is that bad. I suppose I can understand why, because there have been a lot of scandals and mis-selling does go on. And as well as that, a lot of people's only experience with timeshare is with the OPCs ('outside people catchers') – the sales people on the streets with the scratchcards who try to persuade punters to go to a resort for the sales pitch. OPCs can be very pushy and aggressive – they often have to be to get results – and they constantly pester passers-by, which can be a pain. Some of them are perfectly pleasant, but you do get more than a normal share of misfits doing that job – people who couldn't get other work, either in Spain or at home. The in-house sales teams see themselves as far superior to the OPCs, but they would, wouldn't they?

Despite the constant pressure, I enjoyed a lot of my time in the timeshare game. I worked for Club la Costa for over four years, until July 1998, at three locations along the Costa del Sol. I miss the money and I sometimes miss the buzz, but it is a lot more civilised working for the bookshop. And I was ready for a change, having had enough of sales.

Making A Break

My experience with the health service has been very mixed, although I know some people who sing its praises to the sky, particularly compared with Britain's beleaguered health system. I had a bad burn on my arm recently and the care I have had for that has been excellent, but I had a rather different experience when I fractured my elbow. In fact, it was something of a long-drawn-out disaster. It took three and a half months before anybody even recognised that I had fractured my elbow. And during that time I saw four doctors and a consultant and had eight X-rays. This was at the Costa del Sol hospital in Marbella.

Even then, it was a chiropractor who told me first that I had a fracture, but he was the first person actually to examine me properly and touch my elbow. By that time, it looked likely that I wouldn't get back the full use of my arm, such was the length of the delay in treating me. So physiotherapy was deemed to be an emergency, in order to try to help me regain proper use of my arm. But even though it had been declared an emergency, I didn't get the treatment for a month. And that was only after I had been involved in a radio programme about the level of service in the health sector, which somebody at the hospital must have heard or been told about.

It seems to be down to luck, to some extent, as to who sees you and how competent and diligent they are. But that is probably the case in most countries.

I think that what people miss most about their home country is people. But my family visit regularly, so I don't have that problem. I probably have at least one relative coming out every two months or so. When I first moved here ten years ago, there weren't many facilities for foreigners and I missed a decent British book shop, for example. But we have most things now. So the only things I miss about the UK are the rich green countryside and, sometimes, the rain, especially in July and August, when it's so hot, dry and dusty here.

> *when I came to give my version of the accident, they didn't even bother to write it all down*

I think a lot of the best things about living on the Costa del Sol stem from the weather. When it is warm and sunny, as it usually is here, you feel healthier and happier, and you can live an outdoor life. In Britain, the bad weather means people are cooped up in front of the telly for a lot of the time, which isn't the best, most sociable way to live your life.

If I ever left, it would have to be to another warm place. I like the sound of Barcelona, although I haven't been there, and I enjoy Madrid. And I have thought about what it would be like in Portugal. It seems to be cleaner and more relaxed, with friendly locals. I have also heard that it is more upmarket than here – more professional – and you get more refined expats.

The Costa del Sol isn't as pleasant as when I first arrived. It is dirtier and ugly in parts – a bit rough and ready. They don't seem to be spending as much money on the facilities as they should, including the beaches, which are often a mess. And there is a growing drugs culture, which will become a big problem. People have always smoked a bit of pot here but heroin use is really increasing.

Rights & Expectations

That applies to the Costa del Sol in particular, but Spain in general also has its problems for foreign residents. The red tape is one of them. The authorities seem to be obsessed with making everything as hard as possible with regard to permits and all legalities. You find this in so many aspects of life. Some of it is probably the army of civil servants justifying their jobs and existence.

I also don't like the lack of customer service in Spain. You sometimes think their motto is 'The customer is always wrong'. Maybe it's because the wages are often low, so people don't give a monkey's about doing the job well. Another grizzle is that, if a foreigner ever has a problem, accident or disagreement with a Spaniard, he is stuffed – the Spaniard will win. Forget about the idea that we are all Europeans together and equal in all of each other's countries!

To give an example, I had a minor car accident once, involving a Spaniard. The incident was clearly his fault, but when the police turned up and started talking to him, they said something like, "Don't worry, it'll be sorted," meaning "she's a foreigner, she'll get blamed." They didn't realise I spoke Spanish and, when I objected, they didn't know what to say. Despite that, when I came to give my version (the correct one), they didn't even bother to write it all down. So if you need to take up anything legal with a Spanish person, you will have problems.

> *turnover of foreigners is high,*
> *because living here isn't always*
> *as easy as people expect*

To anybody who's thinking of coming here to work, I would say look very carefully at the average wage and working day. The first is lower and the second is longer than in many other European countries. And if you will have to take on staff, it is expensive to pay their social security and they have strong rights. If you are going to work for somebody else, don't expect to get a long contract with full rights because they are rarely given out these days. Newcomers should also be careful when buying a home or a business. Check what is being sold to you and be careful of conmen. And learn Spanish.

More younger people are coming out to Spain than when I started in the book shop. Then, the average customer was over sixty; now a lot are between thirty-five and fifty. But many of them don't stay here for more than a couple of years. Turnover of foreigners is high, because living here isn't always as easy as people expect.

Close Encounters

A former furniture designer, Steve Williams
moved from London to Campo Mijas, since when
he has bought property illegally, had his business
closed down by the police and feared for his
life in the Axarquia mountains.

My brother and I came to Spain to be our own bosses, to live in a warm, relaxed environment and to see what life in another country was like. Settling in was pretty easy, as we knew the area well after holidaying here many times, and the fact that my mum, dad and two brothers were living here helped a lot. Missing the family may be one of the major difficulties that people have after emigrating, but I certainly didn't have that problem. In fact, I saw more of them than I had in the UK. And as soon as we arrived, I threw myself into setting up a new business, so there wasn't much time for moping around, wiping my fevered brow and wondering whether I was settling in properly or not.

Auction Fever

We had bought a restaurant in Campo Mijas on the Costa del Sol without any problems, but it was a different story when we tried to purchase an adjacent building – one that illustrates how you can get into trouble when buying property in Spain, even if you follow all the rules and try to take every precaution to protect yourself from being conned or ripped off.

Next door to the restaurant were three vacant building units, which are known as *locales* in Spanish. We didn't think too much about them until about four years after we had bought the restaurant. Then, one day while we were preparing food for the evening, there was a knock on the kitchen door and two men came in – an older man in a suit and a younger chap with long hair, both respectable-looking – and asked if we wanted to buy a *locale*. It was completely out of the blue and unprompted. We said no and they left.

We didn't think any more about it for a while, but it had made us curious and we went to the administration office of the urbanisation to ask who owned the three *locales*. We were told that a company had originally bought them but had gone out of business quite soon afterwards and the properties had therefore accrued debts, for community fees, *basura* (rubbish collection) and other things. So they had been embargoed in order to reclaim the debts owing before they could be sold, which is standard practice in these circumstances. (It might be a bit more complex than that legally, but this is the general idea.)

Shortly afterwards, we found out that the three properties were going to be auctioned at Mijas Town Hall in order to clear the outstanding debts. A notice was issued to the owners, who were in Madrid, giving them ten days' warning of this, as is also standard practice. We went to the *subasta* (auction) with a translator, intending to buy one of the *locales* to give ourselves more room in the restaurant. As you are recommended to do, we had set a price limit, above which we weren't prepared to go. When the first property came up for sale, the bidders quickly boiled down to just us and a property developer and, when our ceiling price was reached, we had to let him buy it. The same thing happened with the second one and we had to let that go too.

When it came to the third property, we really wanted to buy because it was our last chance to get one of them. Again it came down to us and the property developer and, when our ceiling was again reached, we thought we had missed out. But the person bidding for us got a bit carried away by things and continued to bid! It is apparently quite a common phenomenon, known as 'auction fever', when the excitement of bidding makes people bid higher than their original maximum price. We got the *locale* but had to pay over our agreed ceiling price. Fortunately, it was only a little bit over – about 100,000 pesetas, which was around £250 if I remember the old conversion rate correctly. So it worked out very well in the end. Thank goodness for auction fever – or so we thought at the time.

We bought the *locale* in the early summer and began to renovate it as a seating extension to the restaurant the following September. Things rolled along happily until 23rd December, when we were holding the daytime Christmas party of one of our regular customers. We were starting to clear up when a Spanish man from Cordoba came up the steps of the restaurant and started to rant about the *locale*, saying that we had no right to have done work on it because it wasn't our property, it was his.

> *it reminded me of the astonishing rates of interest charged by the type of moneylenders who break bones if people miss payments*

We told him that we had papers to prove that we had bought it fair and square, but he continued insisting that it was his and looked as if he might get aggressive, so we had to close the gate and lock him out. He calmed down soon after that but, as you can imagine, we were worried by this and went to the Town Hall to explain what had happened and try to clarify the matter. At first, they said that there was nothing to worry about. But they soon changed their story and said that it hadn't actually been their property to sell in the first place!

All's Well That Ends Well

They offered to reimburse us the money we had spent on buying the place but, when we told them about the additional expense of the renovation we had done, they merely shrugged their shoulders, refusing to pay for those too.

Surprisingly, the reimbursement money from the Town Hall came through quickly, but we were still in a difficult position. Then the actual owner – the guy who had ranted at us just before Christmas – said that we could buy the property from him if we wanted.

He told us the price he was looking for, which was rather more than the price we had paid at the auction. We told him this and he said that he was only asking for the current market price, which he was. There was then some amicable negotiating, he accepted that the situation wasn't our fault and that we had spent money on the renovation in good faith, and agreed on a figure that was less than the current market price but more than we had paid originally.

The Town Hall had made the same mistake with the two *locales* bought by the property developer whom we had been bidding against. But the owner from Cordoba refused to sell the *locales* to him, because he said that, whereas we had been decent about a difficult situation, the developer had got nasty with him. So he had dug his heels in and refused to sell, although the developer had done quite a lot of work on at least one of the *locales*.

The two lessons to be learned from this situation are: first, don't trust Spanish Town Halls to have much idea about what they do and don't have the right to sell; and second, don't lose your cool when dealing with agitated men from Cordoba. If you are reasonable with them, they are likely to be the same with you.

Unexpected Bills

We have found that unexpected property-related bills, both for our home and for our business premises, have a habit of arriving regularly – usually at just the wrong time. At least three years after we bought our house, an official letter arrived from the Town Hall, including a bill for €800. It turned out that when we had bought the house, there had been an under-valuation of the property, so we hadn't paid enough tax on the purchase. We assumed that this was the Town Hall's fault, but we still had to pay the difference.

 our concierge certainly isn't the brightest creature alive; stories of his lack of brainpower are legion

But what amazed us most was that from the day we signed for receipt of the letter at the post office – it's like a recorded delivery, but you have to pick it up yourself – there was a daily increase in the amount we had to pay. And because we weren't sure what the letter was about when we picked it up and had to investigate the matter, it took us two weeks after receipt to pay it. By then, the €800 had risen to €1,000! It reminded me of the astonishing rates of interest charged by the type of moneylenders who break bones if people miss payments. But this was the Town Hall, charging through the nose for a bill that was due to their original mistake, and which had taken them three years to get round to resolving!

Believe it or not, in the same week as the bill mentioned above was paid, we received another, also for €1,000 – and this was just before Christmas, when you least want unexpected bills. It had to do with our cafeteria, which was rented. The previous tenant was an Italian, who we didn't really get on with. This was partly because, when you buy a *traspaso* (a sort of right to rent), the landlord receives ten per cent of the transaction fee, which the tenant has to pay. This is standard practice, but the Italian seemed unhappy with it, even though it had nothing to do with us, and it got us off on a bad footing with each other. When he left, he pretty much cleared the place out, which he shouldn't have done, and left us with very little. That soured relations further.

One of my brothers was working with me at the café at the time and he and the Italian were due to go to the electricity company office to change the café electricity account from his name to ours. But they fell out because of the history between us, so the Italian refused to go. We didn't think anything much about it at the time, assuming that the bills would be delivered to us anyway, albeit in the wrong name: we would pay them and there wouldn't be any problem; we could change the name at our leisure.

However, we didn't receive three electricity bills running (they normally come every two months) and one day the power went off. We didn't think much about it because power cuts are quite common here. But when it continued for a while, I asked our neighbouring business if they had power and they said yes. When I approached the building's *portero* (concierge) to see if there was a problem, he blithely said that we had been cut off by the electricity company for not paying the bills. It turned out that the electricity company had been sending them, but the concierge hadn't been delivering them to us because they weren't in our name! When we remonstrated with him, he just grunted and shrugged. So we had to pay the outstanding bill, plus interest and reconnection charges, which came to €1,000, in order to have our power restored.

Our concierge certainly isn't the brightest creature alive; stories of his lack of brainpower are legion. For example, he once noticed a drip from a pipe leading from a business a couple of doors down from us and stuck a piece of chewing gum to the pipe to stop it dripping. But it was meant to drip because it was the outflow of the business's air-conditioning system. Once the pipe was blocked, the water backed up and started leaking into the premises!

Big Brother

When you start a business in Spain, you have to get various licences and permits and have checks made before you can trade – officially speaking anyway. But when we bought the restaurant, we were told that, as long as we had applied for what we needed to apply for, we could start trading while we waited for all the paper to be shuffled – it was an unwritten rule. It is a good job because the wheels tend to move slowly in Spain and you can wait quite a long time to get all the paperwork you need, which can be costly if you aren't trading in the interim.

So, when we came to open the café, we thought that the same would apply, but it proved to be a bit more complicated than that. The first problem was that different inspectors were telling us different things. The first one came round and said that most things in the café were fine, but we just needed to install this and alter that before we would be given the okay to open formally; she would come round in a couple of weeks to check that we had complied with her requests.

Fine, we thought, and did the work. But a couple of weeks later, a different inspector came round: he okayed what we had done but said that we also needed to do a couple of other things! We would have been fine if the original person had come round again, but she didn't and we just had to deal with the extra requiremenbte it in the book and this could mean that your licence to trade is reviewed or revoked. Big Brother is watching you and he is the general public. We would be able to get the forms to apply for a complaints book once our opening licence had come through and that was now being processed because we had had the all-clear from the inspectors.

So we continued to trade, which is unofficially allowed.

One day, two Spanish women came into the café and ordered coffees and then proceeded to take out and eat two cakes which they had bought elsewhere. My brother naturally objected to this but they pooh-poohed him, so he took away their coffees and asked them to leave, which they did. Two days later, however, they came back; when my brother noticed them, he said he wouldn't serve them and also refused one of them permission to use the toilet. They said they would make life difficult for us and left, and they kept their word by denouncing us to the police.

The police came round and we told them the story. They said that the women would need to complain formally and asked where our complaints book was. Of course, we didn't have one and, when we told the police this, they said that we had two alternatives. One was to continue trading and stay open, but if the women decided to be awkward, which seemed very likely, and came back to demand the complaints book and we didn't have one, the police would have to come back and close us. We would then have to begin the whole process of applying to open a business from scratch.

> 66 *one of us would have to reverse along a horribly narrow track, with no barrier and who-knows-how high above the valley floor below* 99

The other alternative, which they recommended we take, was to close while we waited for the complaints book to arrive. We did, but we had to close for four weeks, because that was how long it took to process matters at the Town Hall, even with our *gestor* regularly going up there to chivvy things along. I have to say, though, that the police were fantastic in dealing with what to them must have seemed a petty incident.

Cliff-Hanger

People who live inland from the coast look down their noses at those of us who dwell near the shining, briny sewer that is the Mediterranean. They think of the coast as resembling Reading in a heatwave, polluted by burger joints, British pubs flogging draught beer and satellite TV, tacky souvenir shops and all the rest of the clichéd picture. They aren't far wrong, of course. So, every now and again, I try to get away from the coast and head inland to experience the 'real' Spain.

I had met an interesting British couple on a flight from the UK, who owned an isolated property in the hills of the wild Axarquia region, which is between Malaga and Granada and was, until quite recently, bandit territory. He is an artist and lives there full time, while she commutes to and from the UK, where she works as a child therapist. Most interestingly, they make their own sweet wine, in commercial quantities, most of which is sold in the UK.

One fine spring day, a friend and I decided to accept their open invitation to visit their house on the hill. We drove happily along the coastal motorway, skirted north of Malaga on the new ring road and arrived at Torre del Mar on the eastern Costa del Sol in good time. As instructed, we then turned inland and began to head for our acquaintances' eyrie-like property in the hills.

The journey was fine for a while, but the further inland we went, the rougher the roads became. The road surfaces began to break up, potholes became more frequent, the barriers at the side of the roads became more primitive, before disappearing altogether, and finally a two-lane road became a single track with occasional passing places. All the time, we were climbing higher and higher, and the drops to the valleys below were becoming steeper and deeper.

> *our hosts warned us about one local 'character' who apparently used to stand in the road not wearing trousers or underwear*

We began to feel a bit nervous, grateful that other traffic was almost non-existent and that the weather was fine. By now, we were in high mountain territory, driving along single lane, dried mud tracks, sometimes barely wide enough for the car and with stupendously steep drops, sometimes on both sides, and not a barrier to be seen. Flashes of panic began to appear in our minds. What if we met another vehicle coming the other way? One of us would have to reverse along a horribly narrow track, with no barrier and who-knows-how high above the valley floor below. No thanks!

We were in a big four-wheel drive jeep, which was ideal for the rough terrain but which also had a distinct disadvantage: when you are so high off the ground, you can see over the precipitous mountain edges all the more clearly. We were terrified. At least I had the driving to concentrate on, but my friend was rapidly losing his nerve. The poor chap isn't very good with heights at the best of times, and this wasn't the best of times. I think it was all he could do to stop himself whimpering like a distressed puppy. By the end of the journey the quivering wreck was practically in my lap, so keen was he to try to get away from his side of the car, which had spent the last couple of hours hanging over a cliff.

I am not quite sure how we managed to get to the house in one piece, but we did. And we were shaking when we arrived – literally. I didn't think that actually happened. We both necked a beer like Homer Simpson and gradually began to calm down, while enjoying the hospitality of our slightly eccentric, artistic hosts.

Eerie Eyries

I said earlier that their house was eyrie-like, and I wasn't wrong. It was perched on top of its own hill, and the neighbours were similarly positioned, on the tops of a range of hills that ran as far as the eye could see, hundreds of metres away from each other. It was quite a contrast with the sardine-like packing of property on the concrete Costa.

As well as grapes, they grew almonds, and their crops covered the hill which swept below the house. The shower was outside the house and they seemed to use it quite happily even when they realised that one of their neighbours would watch them through a telescope from his eyrie a couple of hundred metres away. They lived in a little world of their own – geographically and probably psychologically too. My friend and I could easily picture them running naked through their almond groves and vines at midnight, barking at the moon and worse. But we need eccentrics like them.

We enjoyed an excellent lunch of roast lamb and a bottle of wonderful Pesquera 1990 from Ribera del Duero. I couldn't drink much, my mind conscious of the fact that we had to drive back, along those excuses for roads. Fortunately, there was an easier, safer return route, so we were considerably less terrified. And it gave us the chance to drive through the local village, if that is the right word for it. It looked more like a badly-built collection of 18th century homesteads that had suffered an earthquake. And our hosts had warned us about one local 'character' who apparently used to stand in the road not wearing trousers or underwear: marrying first cousins just isn't a sound genetic move.

You won't be surprised to hear that we haven't driven there since. If our friends can lay on a helicopter, we might revisit them, but otherwise, we will stick to meetings at nice safe sea level. But that wasn't our only exposure to the thrill of driving on unguarded mountain roads.

Some Danish friends have moved to the inland town of Competa. It is quite a large, established town and you would imagine that its road links with the coast would be at least adequate. But some of the roads leading there are actually pretty awful – not as bad as those on the way to the Axarquia, but still scary in parts. So the drive there was less than relaxing, particularly for my friend who doesn't like heights. He had to shut his eyes for half the journey to Competa in order to block out the steep drops, potholes, lack of barriers and nutty Spaniards trying to weld their bonnets to our boot. If you don't like driving on twisting, turning, unguarded mountain roads, on which mist can descend with little, if any, notice, it might be best to stick to the flat, coastal bits of Spain.

Foreigners In Spain

You obviously get different opinions from different Spaniards, but one I talk to regularly – he runs a nearby business – has strong opinions about different nationalities living in his country. He thinks the British are no problem at all, that Spaniards and Brtions co-exist easily, although we tend not to integrate into Spanish life and have carved our own unique way of life here. Rather surprisingly, isn't keen on Argentineans, and there are plenty of those coming here since Argentina's economic problems over the last couple of years.

You would think fellow Hispanics would get on, but some Spaniards see Argentineans as arrogant, regarding themselves as better than everybody else. And with so many of them coming to Spain, I think the locals must be feeling rather overwhelmed, as I suppose the British would if herds of Australians suddenly descended on Britain. But from talking to an Argentinean girl who used to work for me, I think part of the problem is that the Argentineans don't like Andalusians, thinking them to be primitive and unsophisticated. The girl concerned moved to Barcelona specifically because she though the people there would be more to her liking – and they apparently are.

Swedes are sometimes regarded as a bit dour or miserable by the Spanish, although a young Swedish employee of ours agrees that the older generation of Swedish people can come across like that, as well as seeming arrogant and having a superiority complex. Germans aren't popular with the Spanish either, but most local vitriol is saved for North Africans, pejoratively called *Moros* (Moors) or, worse, *semillas malas* (bad seeds).

For me, the best things about living here are the climate, the relaxed attitude to things and the emphasis on the family. Not so good are the timeshare touts, the English tourists in football shirts, rip-off English 'craftsmen' and, of course, estate agents. Regarding English 'craftsmen', I recommend that people use Spanish builders. We have been very happy with the extensive work they have done for us, and at half the cost quoted by English builders for the same work. Overall, despite its detractors, the Costa del Sol is a pretty good place to live.

I really enjoy going to watch the football in Spain and often go to Malaga. Most aspects of the football culture here are great and, because there is no tradition of fans travelling to away games, there is very little tension at the grounds. The exceptions are when fans from Seville's two clubs, Sevilla and Real Betis, come. There aren't usually many of them but there is fierce rivalry and it brings out the worst in the hotheads. It doesn't happen often, but I have seen a group of Malaga supporters throwing rocks and flares at a coach carrying fans of one of the Seville teams.

The slight downside to watching football here is the blatant racism of the fans. They do a moronic monkey chant when black players get the ball – even black players on their own side. Then they laugh uproariously at their supposedly clever and hilarious antics. A friend of mine wrote to the club about it and they did acknowledge the problem and said that they were trying to stamp it out, but that there wasn't really too much that they could do, because it was a wider problem for society to address. Apart from this, however, I really enjoy the Spanish football experience.

> *stick to doing what you know and try to learn a little Spanish. And get a good* **gestor** *to handle all paperwork and red tape*

For people considering emigrating to Spain my advice is to make sure that you can afford to live here, because it is more expensive than it used to be. Ask yourself whether you will earn enough to cover your costs. Stick to doing what you know and try to learn at least a little Spanish. And get a good *gestor* to handle all paperwork and red tape.

Mixed Feelings

Louise Cockburn moved with her boyfriend
Graeme from Kent, England, to the Costa del Sol.
Although settled, she now wonders whether it is
the best place for them to live.

We didn't leave Britain because we were unhappy there, but because we thought we might be happier somewhere else, and thought we should have a go at living abroad. Like a lot of younger expatriates, we came to Spain because parents (mine) had a holiday home here. That is why we chose to come to the Costa del Sol rather than anywhere else in the country: we knew the area after visiting on holiday and had a place to stay for free.

My boyfriend, Graeme (who was later to be my husband), wanted to write and so we needed somewhere less expensive than London to live while he worked at that. And back in the mid-1990s, it was much cheaper and quieter here than it is now. We knew our money would go a lot further than it would in the UK and it was a more relaxed environment in which to work. The weather was also an attraction, after we had endured one of the wettest, most depressing British winters for years.

A Quizzical Attitude

We found moving here very easy. But we had visited several times, at different times of the year, and knew some people, and that obviously made things easier. Both our families came out to stay for the first Christmas and that really helped too, because the festive season is probably the time when people who are away from home feel the most homesick. I would advise everybody who is emigrating either to return home for their first Christmas away or to bully family and/or friends into joining you. Going away for the festive season seems to be a lot more popular in Britain than it used to be, so tap into that. But advise people not to travel in the few days leading up to Christmas because airfares really rocket then. It is cheaper to come out before 18th December, or earlier if possible.

To make integrating into life in Spain easier, we made a decision not to get international satellite or cable TV, as so many people do. We were conscious that in the UK, like a lot of people, we had watched too much TV and were over-reliant on it for our entertainment. So we resolved to be different in Spain and saw ourselves spending a lot of evenings out socialising; those that we did spend at home would be taken up by reading great works of literature or watching Spanish TV to improve our language skills. How naïve and idealistic we were back then!

The reality is that when you live somewhere rather than take a holiday there, you can't go out every night because it is too expensive; you don't want to anyway. So TV is a good back-up form of entertainment. But we quickly discovered that Spanish telly isn't very good at all, certainly not one of the country's strengths. Their news programmes and some of the sports coverage are decent, but much of the rest is rubbish: cheap game shows, celebrity gossip magazine programmes and old-fashioned comedies that are as funny as root canal work. So we began to pine for British TV, which is almost certainly the best in the world.

I can remember how excited we were when we discovered that we could get two free foreign channels on our TV: Sky News and a travel channel. We became very well informed about world events because the news was frequently on during the long winter nights, and we clung to watching programmes on the travel channel that we wouldn't normally have dreamed of giving the time of day to when we had had 'proper' telly back in England. I can remember some particularly cheesy travel documentaries made by an Australian called Greg Grainger, which were sometimes verging on the parody – Alan Partridge, without meaning to be.

Our resolve about television has failed spectacularly since those early days in Spain and we now have as many foreign TV channels as we can get. I think the fact that foreigners can receive their home television programmes here is one of the reasons why so many come out. It cushions the impact of being away from home and the strangeness of living in a new country.

I am mildly horrified that we spent time doing something that sounds so naff and train spotter-like

But before we had access to mega multi-channel television, and when we got tired of Sky News and obscure documentaries by gauche Australians on the travel channel, we used to listen to the mixed cocktail that is expatriate radio. I say 'mixed' because it is an unusual blend of the rather good, the adequate and the hopelessly amateurish and often over keen. And at the risk of sounding like somebody at an AA meeting, we became addicted to the quizzes which filled the airwaves back then.

The same couple of dozen people always seemed to dominate these quizzes, clogging the radio stations' switchboards in their eagerness for glory. They obviously spent too many evenings with an encyclopaedia in one hand and the other poised over the phone's quick dial button. On offer was a heady range of potential prizes, including T-shirts, vouchers for meals at restaurants that had to resort to offers to attract custom, cash prizes of two thousand pesetas (a tempting £8!) and free dog food. You can see the attraction!

Taking part must have been the reason for our getting involved, rather than these paltry prizes, but we knew that it was getting out of hand when we began regularly phoning some of our neighbours and friends to compare notes on answers, particularly if there was an unusually chunky prize on offer. And we did once hit the jackpot, winning two nights at a very good hotel. But with hindsight, I am mildly horrified that we spent time doing something that sounds so naff and train spotter-like. Get a life! Fortunately, the 'addiction' didn't last long and we shook ourselves out of the parochial bubble.

Finding A Space

Looking back, it's interesting to remember what struck us as strange and different about life in Spain when we first arrived. It wasn't so much the big, obvious things, like the language, the weather and being in a small seaside town rather than a big city. Rather, it was much smaller, everyday things. One that I remember noticing was Spanish people's different sense of personal space on the beach. If there is a line of sun beds and parasols to choose from, British people will tend to leave as much space as they can between themselves and the nearest other occupants – they will choose the beds furthest away from anybody else. Perhaps it is an extension of our reserve. But the Spanish are the complete opposite and if there is a line of ten beds, for example, and only the one on the far right is occupied, they will come and sit right next to that one.

The same happens in cafés, bars and restaurants – people herd and huddle together, and it can feel claustrophobic for us standoffish northerners, who are used to more space around us. I don't know why the Spanish do it – perhaps it is because several generations of a family often still live together in the same property, cheek by jowl. And a lot of Spanish people live in apartments, on top of each other, so they are used to it; relish it, in fact.

> *we had assumed we would want somewhere quiet and green, out of town, but we found we missed the buzz*

Renting decent property in Spain was easy when we first arrived and that also aided our integration and settling in, because it helps if you have a decent, affordable place to live. We had kept a property in Kent, which we rented out, because we didn't want to cut all ties with England, and we rented here for a few years, to make sure it suited us. As with many things in Spain, we found our first rental through word of mouth, after staying in my parents' place for about three months. We had to move out of there because they wanted to come out for the winter months.

Quite a lot of things are done by word of mouth here – the old adage 'it's not what you know, it's who you know' applies. One of the regulars at a restaurant we used to go to was renting out his neighbour's apartment for him, and that became our first apartment. It was a very good price (partly because the landlord saved on the ten or fifteen per cent agent's letting fee) in a decent location and we stayed there for two years, so we had some stability.

Then we rented a house for three years, which was in the suburbs and again at a competitive price, before renting a flat in the centre of town for eight months to see whether we liked living right in the middle of things. We did and have since bought a house in town, but the only way to tell if an area suits you is to live there for a decent while and we recommend that people try different locations before committing to buy.

We were surprised where we found that we liked living best. We had assumed we would want somewhere quiet and green, out of town, but we found we missed the buzz and liked to have bars, restaurants, taxis and cinemas within walking distance. And because my husband works from home on his own, he likes to be able to nip out to see people, which is much easier when you live in town rather than being stuck out in the boonies.

For our first property rental, we didn't have a contract, but it all ran smoothly, we being decent tenants and the landlord being fair with repairs, etc. With the other places we rented, however, we did have contracts and I would recommend that you do because everybody knows where they stand then. We found that the rental market began to change about three years ago. Rents went up quite considerably and landlords were suddenly less keen to give out long-term contracts, which is what you want for stability – it's a real pain to have to keep moving, particularly if you have to have phones installed each time, which is expensive in Spain.

I think a lot of landlords now want a six-month rental from around November to Easter and to rent short-term for the rest of the year because they can charge a lot during the beach holiday season and make more over a year, even if they don't have full occupancy. So renting isn't as easy or cheap as it was. In fact, one of the reasons we rented here for so long is that it was cheap and easy, allowing us to continue renting out our property in Kent for much more than we were paying here, at the same time as it was increasing in value.

But I wonder if the rental market here will change soon, and again favour the tenant. There has been a shortage of decent rented accommodation over the last few years, but there has been so much new property built recently and more to be finished soon that there look set to be many more properties available for rent. And at the same time, the number of short-term tourists coming to Spain seems to have levelled off, or it might even be falling. So long-term renters might do better here soon. In fact, landlords might be chasing them. And some of those landlords who have been greedy over the last few years might get bitten and have trouble finding tenants to pay their mortgages for them. I can't help laughing!

Estate Agents & Builders

We have only bought once in Spain so we aren't experts, but we found it straightforward. But you have to be careful because there are a lot of sharks around, so get a decent lawyer to check things like the fact that the seller actually owns the property, that there are no imminent plans to build a motorway slip road through your back garden (although you never know what they are going to come up with next here) and that the property doesn't have any outstanding debts attached to it: you as the new owner would be liable for them because they attach to the property and not to the person who ran them up. If you use a decent lawyer, you shouldn't have any problems.

The main thing we object to with regard to the buying and selling of houses in Spain is the fees, charges and taxes associated with it, which are a rip-off: at least ten per cent of the value of the property, sometimes more. The thing that many people seem to object to most is Spanish estate agents' charges. Coming from Britain, where you pay between one and one-and-a-half percent, it is a real shock to discover that Spanish agents charge a minimum of five per cent, often more. In fact, what they sometimes do is to ask you how much you want for a property and then advertise it for a lot more and take any excess above the amount you wanted, which can be ten per cent plus!

A couple of years ago, I remember seeing advertisements for a firm that tried to shake the market up by doing away with these high estate agents' commissions and charging a set fee. They seemed to do well for a while; I don't know what has happened to them since. I recommend that you negotiate strongly with estate agents regarding their commission. They are really struggling at the moment, with far too many chasing too little business in a flattish market. The number of estate agencies in this region has mushroomed over the last five years, although they are starting to close now and I know that two of the biggest, most high profile chains have laid off a lot of agents and support staff.

So estate agents, after several years of greed and plenty, are suffering and are ripe to be beaten down on the amount they earn. They need sales, even if they have to reduce their commission. They have been screwing us all for some years, so let's do the same to them now! What do they do to justify such big fees anyway? List property details, take phone calls and drive people to see properties. Sorry, but it isn't rocket science and therefore shouldn't be a highly paid job.

When you think of the words 'Spanish' and 'builder' together, it might conjure up thoughts of disastrous inefficiency, incompetence and delay. But think again, because our experience has been good. We had two-and-a-half months' building work done on our current home before moving in and have been very happy with it. The work was extensive, involving general labourers, a plumber, an electrician and carpenters: we had two bathrooms completely replaced, the kitchen gutted and replaced, fitted wardrobes built in one bedroom, some floor retiling and the house was completely rewired and re-plumbed, i.e. there was plenty to go wrong and it involved lots of different workers, who had to coordinate their work. Add to that the fact that the labour took place in the summer, which is the hottest time of the year and also the Spanish holiday season, when workers and suppliers take their holidays, meaning potential delays to everything. Despite all that, our experience was very positive.

even though my Spanish isn't bad, I cannot tune my ear to the local way of speaking

The contractor was English-born, but fully integrated into Spanish life and fluent in Andalusian Spanish, and all the workers were Spanish. It is very handy having somebody who speaks English in charge of the work, because when giving complex instructions and making changes, if there is a problem of translation, you can have all sorts of problems and expensive mistakes can be made. But using Spanish workmen seems to be preferable. They work hard, know local techniques and suppliers, and aren't fly-by-nights, as some foreign workers are. Try to use established people, who have a reputation to protect. Local workers also tend to be cheaper. English workmen sometimes want to charge English prices.

What surprised us most was how hard the Spanish guys worked, at the hottest, most punishing time of the year. We expected the *mañana* attitude and the work to take a lot longer than expected, but they turned up every day at 8am on the dot and worked through, with only an hour for lunch, which is unheard of here – two or three hours is usual, especially in the summer. The entire project was finished only a week or two behind schedule, and that was partly because the plumber's father-in-law was taken seriously ill, so his not being there for a few days was perfectly understandable.

Spanish Lessons

We had a home tutor for a year before we came to Spain and that gave us a good basic knowledge of the language before we arrived. But my husband was better than me, so he probably got more out of it. That is apparently unusual though; the teacher said that women are normally better at learning languages than men, perhaps because they aren't as insecure and afraid of making mistakes. And you make a lot of mistakes when learning a foreign language.

But I have found it very difficult to learn the language properly since we have been here. That is a mixture of my laziness, the fact that a lot of foreigners want to speak English and the difficulty of learning a foreign language properly. And such is the accent here that even though my Spanish isn't bad – I can talk on the phone, deal with the bank, etc. – I cannot tune my ear to the local way of speaking, so I cannot always understand people.

> " *some people say things in*
> *front of you that they wouldn't*
> *normally dream of saying in*
> *front of a stranger* "

I attended Spanish classes here for a year. They are run by the local council and, if you are a resident here, you get the lessons cheaper. I only paid about £20 for a term, so cost is no excuse for not taking lessons. The teacher was very nice and competent, and she only ever spoke Spanish, because it was a class of around twenty-five and there were lots of different nationalities: British, Danish, German, Chinese and Moroccan.

Nevertheless, I didn't learn a great deal because of the nature of the classes. Different nationalities have different ideas about timekeeping and quite a lot of people just turned up when they wanted, which disrupted the classes. The teacher used to get cross about people turning up late and not doing their homework, but it didn't seem to have much effect. And some people used to bring their kids to the class, which was a distraction – as was the fact that the teacher usually took at least two phone calls per class and used to leave the class to take them. So it isn't much of a surprise that I didn't learn as much as I had hoped.

Waiting

I took the first year we were here off work, and then began to work in a restaurant as a waitress. It was an upmarket place, in a nice location, run by a British family, who subsequently became friends. We ate there one evening shortly after they took it over and I told them that I would be interested if they needed any help. Initially, I only filled in when they were busy, but I ended up working there six nights a week and did so for five years.

It was a great place to work, with nice people and I was given a proper contract, which gave me access to healthcare and social security. That was rare: a lot of places here prefer to pay cash in hand and not give contracts, because they are expensive (with the social security payments) and give staff rights too. I also got a decent wage and my fair share of tips, but that again is rare. Working conditions in Spain for foreigners aren't always so advantageous.

So I had it relatively easy, whereas a lot of people who work in bars and restaurants here have to deal with some obnoxious customers for little material reward or job security. But working six nights a week has a heavy impact on your social life, particularly when it isn't unusual to work to eleven o'clock at night or midnight. And it gets very hot here during the summer, even at night, which can make working difficult and tiring. Hot weather is an obvious attraction for holidaymakers but it can be a bit of a nightmare for people who have to rush around working in it. Working over Christmas and New Year can be very hard but it is also lucrative, even if you have to watch family and friends enjoying themselves while you ferry turkey, wine and party bags around.

But I generally enjoyed the job and there were few disadvantages. Perhaps one was the fact that outside the main tourist season the level of custom was hit or miss, which meant the hours I worked were uncertain, making it difficult to estimate my income. Nevertheless, we invariably had nice customers and I became friends with my bosses, so I have a rose-tinted view of what working in a Costa del Sol restaurant is like.

The owners employed quite a few young people in the time I was there – mainly British, and mainly as waiters. They had a pretty high turnover of staff, however, which certainly wasn't because it wasn't a nice place to work – quite the reverse, actually – but because they tended to be bad timekeepers or not to show up, and didn't seem to have much sense of responsibility or loyalty. I don't want to generalise too much, but I have heard from a few people that young people brought up here tend to be like that: they drift from job to job, getting by but never pushing themselves. Perhaps it is being brought up in a relaxed, gentle environment. Friends of ours with teenagers are going to send them away to a Spanish or British city when they reach eighteen or nineteen to toughen them up and show them what life is like out of this comfort zone, as one of Graeme's friends describes the Costa del Sol.

One of the lasting memories I have of working in a restaurant used mainly by expats is of how nice many of the foreigners are on the Costa del Sol, because most of our customers were nice people. I know this will surprise some, who think that all British people on the Costas are yobs or criminals. You do get those, I won't deny it, but there are lots of civilised people too.

You overhear interesting things as a waitress. In fact, some people say things in front of you that they wouldn't normally dream of saying in front of a stranger. They seem to think waiters can't hear. I remember an American woman wondering if we sold Chardonnay, to which her husband replied, "Don't be silly, dear; they only make that in America." I was about to tell him that it was a French grape, grown all over the world, but had to bite the bullet. The customer is always right, even when they appear to have learning difficulties.

How The Other Half Lives

I also worked as a cleaner for a while, one morning per week. That again was for a friend, who had a large villa, and I enjoyed it. We used to do the villa together and chatted while we were working. My husband and I also did some villa- and pet-sitting, which was interesting and gave us the chance to live in a variety of large properties for a while, and see which type suited us and what we aspired to. There is quite a demand for reliable house-sitters here, a lot of people having pets and splitting their time between Spain and the UK or wherever.

Our experience of large villas with lots of land is that they have their strengths and their weaknesses. They are probably at their best in the hot weather, between about May and October, when you live outside for a lot of the time. You can enjoy the terraces, gardens and swimming pool and run around with no clothes on if you want. It is good to have your own space and privacy to enjoy the fine weather here. And it is a bonus to have everything you need at home rather than having to go to the beach or an 'aqua park' to find it, along with the tourist hordes. That is especially true from mid-July to mid-September when it is too hot and crowded to venture far from home.

Living on urbanisations with shared gardens and pools, we of course had to share them with holidaymakers and their kids. This is fine if the kids are well behaved, but they usually aren't these days. We also discovered when looking after other people's villas that we would enjoy having a property with some land because it allows you to grow your own fruit and vegetables. The climate here is such that things grow all year and I think I would enjoy having the space to do that. We house-sat one place that had several acres of land, on which grew tomatoes, onions, peppers, chillies and courgettes, as well as there being a couple of dozen avocado trees, which provided almost commercial quantities of fruit. But then, there is only so much guacamole that a person can eat.

There are also downsides to living in large villas. I think you can become isolated in a big property and never even see your neighbours, let alone have the chance to get to know them. And there is the security aspect. It is difficult and expensive to secure the perimeter of a large piece of land and, if somebody breaks through it, they have plenty of time and cover to clear out your home. So that means you have to get alarms and/or guard dogs, which are a responsibility and expense. And if you go away on holiday, you have to make provision and get in reliable house-sitters – just the sort of hassle that people come to Spain to avoid.

Large villas here can be very cold in the winter, much colder than the air outside. The marble that keeps you cool in the summer is pretty bleak in the winter. We stayed in one place with a large, impressive lounge and a minstrels' gallery, which looked great, but the high ceiling made it even harder to heat and the owner spent a small fortune every winter keeping warm.

Jobs like cleaning and house-sitting are things that I wouldn't even have considered doing back in the UK, where I worked in computer systems. But a lot of expatriates end up doing that in Spain, i.e. taking on a few sometimes menial jobs in order to make a living and stay out here. There is a group of expatriates in Spain who make a living serving the wealthier ones – as gardeners, drivers, cleaners, etc. But apart from bar and restaurant work, and doing the odd jobs for other expats, your choice of work here is limited to timeshare or working in a call centre or for an estate agent. It is only in the last year or so that I have found a job that I would have considered doing in the UK: in finance.

Friends & Foreigners

We have found that it has taken a long time to make close friends here. There has been no problem with acquaintances, but to make close friends, you need to meet like-minded people and there is a much, much smaller pool of those on the Costa del Sol than in Britain. I think not having children also makes it more difficult to meet people of your own age; I know that some of our friends and acquaintances say they probably wouldn't see so much of some of their friends if their children didn't know each other.

I don't see much evidence of Spanish and foreign people mixing in this part of the world, let alone becoming close friends. It is mainly the language barrier, rather than because the Spanish aren't good people. They often are and seem pretty tolerant of all the foreigners living in their country. A lot of Spanish people round here accept that they are much better off now than they were before the foreigners arrived.

> *you can still eat and drink well for less than the price of an average round of drinks in a dingy British pub*

But I think that Spanish people can sometimes seem a bit dour, particularly to the British. It reminds me of something Bill Bryson wrote; I can't remember exactly how he put it, but it was something like: 'when you see two Britons together, there's usually a lot of smiling and laughter'. That is less common with the Spanish and I think it is a gulf between the British and them. I also find that people can be rude when you speak Spanish to them and don't quite get it right. They don't seem to make allowances for it not being your native language, although maybe that is an understandable build-up of frustration after having had to deal with so many foreigners who won't try to speak any Spanish.

One of the best things about living here is that you can still eat and drink out quite cheaply, which is very different from London, where I used to live. We really notice this every Sunday, when we often go to a Spanish bar on the seafront to drink beer at less than £1 a glass and eat decent *tapas* which cost just a few quid for enough to fill you up. If you know where to go, you can still eat and drink well for less than the price of an average round of drinks in a dingy British pub. So for people who like dining out, you can do a lot more of that here, even if you are on a budget.

A downside is that in the bars and restaurants on the Costa del Sol you are prey to people coming round selling dodgy CDs and DVDs, fake designer sunglasses, toys and other rubbish. Some days, there is an almost constant stream of these people and it gets pretty tiresome having to say "No" all the time. The number of buskers can be a real bore too, interrupting everybody's conversation with their naff music and expecting to be paid for having forced it on people.

The generally good weather means that you can eat and drink outside for much of the year, certainly at lunchtime. But the weather here isn't as good as a lot of visitors seem to think it will be. When the winter weather is warm and dry, it is the nicest time of the year, but it can be cool and wet for weeks on end, not that some of the holidaymakers seem to realise. Many is the time we have seen people wearing vests and shorts in a stiff breeze and squally rain, seemingly unwilling to accept that it can ever be anything but warm and sunny in a part of the world called the 'sunshine coast'. Some of them obviously think that we have weather like Jamaica, but we don't. It can be odd in the winter to see tourists on the beach in swimsuits, while locals and long-time expats huddle in coats, sometimes scarves – things they rarely have a chance to wear.

Minus Marks

The relaxed way of life in Spain is another plus, although the longer I am here, the more I think it is certainly an advantage if you are on holiday or retired, but perhaps a drawback if you have to work. So it's a mixed blessing.

I don't think a day goes by without my saying 'unbelievable' at some act of stupidity or selfishness by another driver

For example, there are a lot of bank holidays here, and if there is one on a Thursday, people also take the Friday off, to make a long weekend, a so-called *super-puente*. As well as that, they wind down at work in the days prior to the public holidays and take time to wind back up again after them! That is not laid-back so much as lazy and is one of the reasons why things can take so long to get done here.

Another minus about living in Spain is the very poor driving. There is an unwillingness to anticipate problems, people rarely use indicators, they drive at crazy speeds right in the boot of the car in front and they park anywhere. I don't think a day goes by without my saying "unbelievable" at some act of stupidity or selfishness by another driver. Last week we pulled onto the inland, toll motorway, which always has light traffic because it is a pay road: as usual, it was very quiet but, as we pulled on, a lorry that was following overtook us on the inside, on the slip road, and then cut us up so much that we nearly went into the back of him. We sat there open-mouthed and silent, too stunned to react to something so unbelievably impatient, stupid and dangerous.

We dread taking taxis to the airport because it involves a motorway journey, which sometimes scares the life out of us, depending on how reckless the driver is. They invariably drive suicidally close to the car in front, leaving no room for error, while also lighting cigarettes, changing the radio station or cassette and preening themselves in the mirror. To try to counter the speed at which they drive, we took to saying, "We're not in a hurry," but that didn't have much effect. So now we say, "we're early, so please drive slowly." That works better, and we don't have to spend the journey to the airport with our eyes shut.

The primitive, unreliable electricity supply is another minus in southern Spain. In wet and stormy weather, the electricity in many areas goes off, which seems ridiculous in a European country in the 21st century. People sometimes say, "Oh, but it happens in Greece too." It might, but two wrongs don't make a right. And it can be a major problem, not just because of the inconvenience of trying to run a modern home or office without electricity. The power often flickers back on and off a few times before being properly restored, and you sometimes get so-called power surges, which can damage or even destroy any electrical appliances which are plugged in when the surge occurs. You can buy surge protectors, which offer some protection, but they aren't infallible. A bad surge can be very expensive if it blows out several appliances. You invariably have to pay for this, even though it is the electricity company's fault for having a lousy, primitive system. But try proving it to the company, which you will need to do if you want to get compensation. And everybody knows that taking legal action in Spain is a long-drawn-out, inefficient process, which you might lose anyway, even with a strong case. So who is going to take on a massive power company for the sake of a few hundred or even a couple of thousand euros?

I did hear about the residents of one block of apartments who joined together to take on the electricity company *Sevillana*. A particularly large surge had apparently damaged or destroyed dozens and dozens of fridges, TVs, computers and other electrical items in the block, and the overall bill for the damage was large. So the people got together to take a joint legal action against the power company. I think it was settled before it went to court, but it needs that kind of strong-arm tactic to achieve anything.

Another negative is the fact that people spit in the street here. It isn't seen as rude or unhygienic, and I know that people do it elsewhere too, but I still find it disgusting. Even well-dressed, middle-aged people do it – a national character flaw in my opinion, along with the awful driving. Some people explain away these things as 'cultural differences', but I think that is just a wet example of political correctness, in a world that doesn't like to criticise the behaviour of others for fear of being branded a fascist.

The Costa Del Con

I also don't like the dog poo that seems to be everywhere, and the inheritance and property taxes are an unfair rip-off. In fact, rip-offs and cons are my final minus, in what seems like a long list of whinges! The longer we have been here, the more I have come to feel that there are rip-off merchants and conmen on every corner. As well as suffering bank charges for everything, estate agent commission rates five to ten times those in the UK, employment-stifling social security charges and all the other local and national taxes, a stroll down the seafront makes you prey to the hordes trying to sell you timeshare, counterfeit CDs, sunglasses, watches and DVDs, or other things you don't want or need.

You aren't even safe in your own home. A regular scam is tried by people who pose as gas maintenance men and come to 'check the installation', including the piping on the gas bottles that are still used here. (They are soon to introduce mains gas but for now it comes in distinctive orange gas bottles.) The conmen are clever, with uniforms that mimic those of genuine gas company employees and clip boards with genuine-looking paperwork. They gain entry like this and then proceed to make a big thing of checking your gas bottle and the pipe leading from it, even though it is a very simple set-up. While one of them distracts you, the other puts a small cut in the pipe and then makes a big show of it, demonstrating that it must be replaced. This they do, but at a greatly inflated price: they will charge you ten times as much as it would cost you in a supermarket for replacing what that they themselves have damaged. We were approached by such people not long after we arrived, but we had read about them and didn't get caught; we know of people who have been.

As for the timeshare touts, we used to sit in a café near where they congregate, watching them operate and spin their yarns. It was like a free, outdoor cabaret as you watched them go through their patter – and some of them are very good performers. The usual approach seems to be to say that they are doing promotional work or a survey and then to give out scratchcards for the associated prize draw. The tout then makes a big gesture of surprise when it shows that the people have won – even though all the cards are the same – and says that to claim their prize (usually money and/or bottles of Cava or whisky) the people simply have to go to the resort in a cab paid for by the tout and listen to a short, no-pressure presentation. It isn't a short presentation, of course, but can go on for three or four hours, and it is a sleek, high-pressure, hard-sell operation designed to make you buy timeshare, which quite a few people still seem to do.

I know that there are good and bad timeshare operations, but it appears to me always to be an expensive way to pay for future holidays up-front. And you tie yourself to the same place at the same time for years to come. I know that you can swap with others, but why bother with all the faffing around? And the scamming doesn't end when you have bought your timeshare. Some companies make a lot more money by charging very high service fees, which the contract they have signed obliges people to pay.

> *don't rule out the possibility of going back – don't be too proud to admit it was a mistake*

They can also sting you when you decide that you want to sell your timeshare. I heard about one approach which involves convincing people with a week's timeshare which they want to sell that one-week packages don't sell very well and that, if they buy another week to make it a two-week timeshare, it will sell quickly. The poor sap then buys another week, but of course the two-week package doesn't sell either. You have to admire the sales people's imagination if not their ruthlessness.

No Red Tape

There are definitely lashings of red tape and bureaucracy in Spain but I don't think they are as bad as people make out – and things are improving. When we applied for *residencia* (to become residents), we did it ourselves and, although it took some time and involved a certain amount of queuing, it was reasonably straightforward. But we do speak decent(ish) Spanish and couldn't have done it alone if we hadn't. The staff at quite a lot of government offices and police stations speak only Spanish, which slows things up and leads to confusion because a lot of foreigners here don't – and not just the British, I am pleased to say. It would speed things up if there were interpreters or English-speaking staff available and that would help everybody in the queues, both Spanish and foreign.

We also got married in Spain, in a civil ceremony at a Town Hall. It was very well organised: the deputy mayor married us in Spanish, the town hall provided an interpreter to translate the service into English (she was Danish) and the whole ceremony, in the two languages, took about fifteen minutes – no messing. The Town Hall even gave us a present – some engraved glasses – and the ceremony was done free of charge. So I recommend getting married here. When we got married, you had to be official residents of the local borough, but I am not sure if that is still the case. [It is in some boroughs but not others. Ed.] If you get married here between May and October, the weather should be sunny, but it gets very hot here from June to September, so make it a casual affair – no meringue dresses or morning suits, unless you want to melt.

I think our worst experiences of red tape and inefficiency in Spain have been with the traffic department. Transferring ownership of a vehicle can be a nightmare, which you have little control over, and the system really needs amending.

Keeping An Open Mind

If somebody told me that they were considering emigration to the Costa del Sol, I would ask them to think it through properly first. Don't do it simply because you have enjoyed holidays here or like sunny weather. Living in a place is very different from holidaying there, and good weather won't see you through if you find that you don't like much else about the place. If you have property in Britain, Denmark, Sweden or wherever, don't sell it and cut off your potential escape route back. Rent it out instead and make sure that you rent in Spain before buying. And you will find that it is probably easier to make friends if you live in an apartment or a townhouse than in an isolated villa.

a piece of advice to others thinking of emigrating to a sunny region would be to consider other places as well as Spain

Keep an open mind and don't give up too easily if at first you don't like living in Spain. It can take a long time to settle in a new country. But don't rule out the possibility of going back - don't be too proud to admit it was a mistake. View trying a life abroad as an itch that had to be scratched. If you are retired, make sure that you have enough to occupy your time, other than drinking cheap gin and watching videos. If you have a job in Spain, get used to the idea that most of your family and friends who visit will forget this fact and assume that you are on holiday all the time.

If you are serious about living in Spain for the long term, you will need to learn the language quite well. If you can't or don't want to learn it, consider going somewhere English-speaking, like Florida, California, Australia, New Zealand or South Africa. We visited South Africa earlier this year and really liked it. It is similar to southern Spain, with a Mediterranean climate, vineyards, beaches and mountains just inland. But it is been much better developed (or rather, it hasn't been overdeveloped), without the endless stretches of ugly, high-rise concrete buildings that we have on the Costa del Sol.

The Cape Town area of South Africa shows what the Costa del Sol could have been like if it hadn't been so overdone in the concrete department. I think that the trip there unsettled Graeme and me, and made this coast look a bit tired and shabby. We wouldn't move to South Africa because it is too far away from family and friends in Europe, and as well as its attractions the country does have problems, but it highlighted some of the Costa del Sol's weaknesses and made us realise that there are plenty of other sunny places to live.

As for the unceasing building work going on in this part of the world, I thought that it might finally have finished in the area of town where we live and that everybody could at last get some respite from the noise and dust, but I was wrong. Now that apartment blocks and townhouses have been thrown up on every bit of green space available, they have decided to embark on a major programme of road replacement and flood drain improvement. They have also dug up part of the road and pavement near the beach, all of which was completely remodelled only eighteen months ago. It seems endless. So our final piece of advice to others thinking of emigrating to a sunny region would be to consider other places as well as Spain.

Living It Down In Madrid

Christopher Campbell moved from his native
Vancouver to Madrid – via Toronto, New York,
Dublin and London – to train as an architect.
He ended up working as a waiter, tour guide,
fruit picker, proofreader and teacher.

I had always intended to move to Europe and experience living here. My background is Scottish – most of my family live there and I have a British passport. Vancouver is a great place to be brought up and British Columbia is a very beautiful part of the world, but it is quite an outdoorsy sort of life and that isn't really for me. In fact, the city and its surrounds were wasted on me. As well as walking in some great parks, you can ski, sail, hike, climb mountains, fish and canoe – none of which I do! Western Canada can also feel a bit cut off, as can Canada in general, and I wanted to live in the ancient, historic, sophisticated continent of Europe.

I chose to go first to Dublin and London for the shared language, but found Dublin a bit limited and London to be a big, imposing place. The latter has masses of attractions, including the great parks, shops, museums and galleries, but it is expensive and can be unfriendly – not always a fun place for a newcomer without much money.

I took a cheap weekend vacation to Madrid and loved it – it is like a half-way house between Dublin and London, with more to offer than the first but easier to handle than the second – so I made a decision to try living here for a while. When I returned to London I took a part-time TEFL (teaching English as a foreign language) course and a crash course in Spanish, and I moved to Spain a couple of months later. There wasn't much logic or planning behind the decision, just a gut reaction – but I usually go with my instincts in life. I don't actually know why, because they don't always work out!

Time Differences

When I came to live in Madrid, I was prepared for it being massively different from anything I had experienced before, so it hasn't been as much of a shock as I had imagined it would. I had psyched myself up to face a bigger change than it actually proved, so it was easier for me than expected because it isn't like living on a different planet.

It also helped that I have been used to living in different places. After Vancouver, I spent time in Toronto, New York, Dublin and then half a year or so in London, so a new city wasn't a big surprise to me. The obvious and biggest difference I faced was the language barrier because I had only a few months of basic Spanish when I came. But I took Spanish lessons here immediately and learned more of the language quickly. It definitely helps if you have a base to build on before you come, as I did.

My tutor helped in a couple of ways. It was through her that I found the shared apartment I still rent and also my first English-language pupils. She was also my first friend in Spain. So I owe her a lot and was lucky to find her as soon as I arrived because it really helped me to settle in. I think culture shock and homesickness must be a lot worse if you are isolated, but I wasn't and that made a big difference. I was lonelier and more isolated when I moved to London, even though I spoke the same language as the natives.

> " *it is such a late-night culture.*
> *People don't venture out until*
> *10pm . . . you need stamina to get*
> *the best out of life in Madrid* "

But life in Madrid is rather different from what I am used to. That is a good thing, though – why come if it is the same as home? Madrid is a sort of a mixture of the formal and the relaxed. And the hours people keep, especially during the summer, are crazy. It is such a late-night culture. People don't venture out until 10pm, have a drink at a bar, then eat in a restaurant at 11pm or midnight, and then on to more bars or a club in the early hours of morning, before stopping for chocolate and *churros* (a sweetish doughnut-like thing, served in strips) on the way home at 7am!

And they don't just do this on Friday and Saturday nights, when there is no work the next day. If something interesting is happening during the week, like a new bar opening or a special club night, they do it then too and go home afterwards to shower and change before going straight to work after little or no sleep. So you need stamina to get the best out of life in Madrid.

The timekeeping, or rather the lack of it, is also difficult to get used to. Time doesn't mean much in Spain and I was told early on that it is important to realise that when somebody says they will deliver something or come round to repair the boiler *mañana*, it usually doesn't actually mean 'tomorrow', but 'not today'. That is an important lesson to learn here and life is easier if you just try to accept it and arrange your life accordingly.

You also have to try to attune your ear when somebody says they will do something at a certain time, to gauge how much uncertainty is in their voice and so how long it is likely to take. I haven't managed to get it right yet. But with my students, time-keeping hasn't been a problem. Most of them are keen to learn so they turn up on time. And besides that, the lesson times are fixed and paid for in advance: if they don't turn up, I still get paid, which is the important thing.

Football Fanaticism

I live in a shared flat with two other guys – one Spanish, the other Argentinean – and that also helped me to settle in quickly. I was rarely alone; I got to meet their friends and they took me out with them. Luckily, the three of us got on from the start and, although they both speak pretty good English, we usually speak Spanish, which helped me to learn, although we speak more English now because they want to improve their English.

They think a Canadian accent is easier to understand than some of the British accents they hear. But I find some British accents and slang impossible to understand too, especially some of the things my Scottish family comes out with. In fact, most Spanish people assume I am British because there are so many Britons in Spain, while most British people think I am American, but Canadians are used to that. I am told that it is the same for New Zealanders – everybody thinks they are Australians.

A new interest for me in Spain has been soccer, or football as it is called in Europe, but I haven't had much choice about that. Both of my flat mates are fanatical supporters and it is the same with a lot of Spaniards and Hispanics. Not all of them, as people sometimes think, but a lot. The best-selling daily papers in this country by far aren't actually newspapers, but sports papers, dealing mainly with football. My flat mates talk about the game constantly and we watch a great deal of football on television: Spanish League, English League and the Champions' League, which is a club tournament for the best teams in Europe.

They talk endlessly not just about the games and the players, but also about the underlying appeal of the game – it is that ingrained in them. One of them, the Spanish guy, maintains that football's appeal to so many men is that it recreates the thrill of the ancient hunt, which we have lost in modern life. Instead of stalking mammoth, bison and deer, as our forebears did, we go to supermarkets and *tapas* bars to feed ourselves and our families. Football, apparently, is a substitute for the excitement of the ancient group hunts, with the attacks on goal representing the attacks on the animals. And as was the case that most individual attacks on animals were unsuccessful, most attempts on goal are too.

 the Madrid climate has been described as 'nine months of winter and three months of hell'

The Argentine goes even deeper, seeing football as a religion substitute. According to him, a gathering of 100,000 people (the approximate capacity of the Bernabeu, Real Madrid's impressive stadium) in an outdoor football stadium is the modern equivalent of the ancient gatherings at stone circles and other prehistoric sites. The crowd are the worshippers and the players represent ancient priests, while the goalkeeper is apparently the holiest of them, because he guards what is the equivalent of the gateway to the underworld, the goalmouth. I leave others to decide if there is anything to this, or if it is simply pretentious European and South American moose-shit.

I suppose foreigners often think that the Spanish religion is Roman Catholicism and the national sport is bullfighting. But that is wrong – the religion and national sport are the same, football. I have quite a few British and Irish friends in Madrid and many of them are obsessed with the game too. If they aren't watching it or talking about it, they are playing it, usually five-a-side. I have played a few times but I usually end up in goal because I am not very good. But playing sport is a good way to meet people and settle into a new place.

Culture & Climate

There are plenty of English-speaking foreigners in Madrid and getting to know some of them can help you to settle in, as well as being a useful source of tips about the city. I avoided mixing with other English-speakers when I first arrived because I wanted to integrate with Spanish people. But recently, I have got to know quite a few other foreigners and enjoy their company, sometimes in the city's Irish bars. Wherever I have travelled, Irish bars always seem to be popular gathering places. So if you are lonely in a new town, seek one out. Their friendly atmosphere means that you will usually find plenty of people to talk to.

Another difference I have noticed in Spain is the attitude to alcohol. Parts of Canada and Britain have a big drinking culture and a lot of people's social lives involve a great deal of boozing. But it is different here. People rarely drink alcohol to excess and sometimes have soft drinks if they aren't eating. I know that the Spanish are amazed by the amount that some foreigners drink, especially some Irish guys I know, who have an astonishing capacity for beer. But Spaniards are introduced to alcohol at an early age, so it isn't a novelty to them. You do see young people gathering on street corners at night to drink cheap wine, but public drunkenness in adults is rare. Drugs, however, are quite a big problem in Madrid, but that is the case in most big cities these days.

I think that part of the reason I have settled in so well is that I really like Madrid. It isn't a typical capital city because, despite having some great museums and galleries, which you expect in a capital, it also has a provincial feel to it and isn't as large or hectic as some capital cities. So you get a lot of the facilities without too much of the craziness. And if you live near the center, like me, you can walk most places, unlike in London or New York, which are too big.

I also like the weather, which comes as a surprise to some people. The Madrid climate has been described as 'nine months of winter and three months of hell', meaning that the winters are too long and the summers boiling hot. But I disagree. It can be cold here in the winter, but it is often dry and sunny at the same time, which makes for great socializing and sightseeing weather, and gives you the chance to wear 'proper' clothes – jumpers, jackets, and scarves.

And when I say 'cold', it is nothing like the Canadian definition of cold. I am from Vancouver, which has a mild climate, like southern England, but I have spent winters in Toronto and that is real cold. You rarely get anything like that here. Best of all, there is a lot less rain in Madrid than in Vancouver, 400mm per year rather than 1,100mm. Some winters in Vancouver, it just seems to rain every day, which is pretty depressing, and summers can be damp too.

The summers can be very hot in Madrid, but it rarely becomes unbearable, because it isn't usually humid, and that is much worse than heat. Besides that, a lot of people leave the city around the third week of July and go to the mountains or the coast for a month or so to escape the heat, so the city has its own quieter charm then. It half-closes between about July 21st and the first week of September, which means no teaching for me and a five- or six-week holiday!

This is unknown to North Americans, who tend to have much shorter holidays. It is very much a European thing and very civilized, although I don't get paid when I don't work so have to work extra hard before and after the break to pay for it. But having so much time off at once really gives people the time to relax properly, which is a good thing.

Back to the weather, which is a subject that people from Vancouver talk about a lot, spring and autumn in Madrid can be wonderful. They are probably the best times to visit, if you are thinking of taking a vacation here.

I also like the culture in Madrid. The galleries, museums, parks, markets and some of the architecture are wonderful, as is the café-style way of life. And you can eat out well and cheaply, which is unusual in a big city and important to somebody like me who doesn't earn a fortune. Madrid isn't Europe's prettiest city, especially the outskirts, but if you stay in the center and enjoy an active, varied social life, it is a great place to live.

The Simple Life

Teaching English as a foreign language has been a revelation to me. It lets you earn a living for working only part-time, allows you to meet a lot of usually open-minded people and is a skill you can take just about anywhere outside the English-speaking world. There is a great demand for English teachers, especially native speakers, because English is the language of so much of the world's business, culture and entertainment. I don't think it is quite as dominant as is sometimes argued and it might have reached its peak, with Mandarin Chinese the language of the mid-21st century onwards, but for now, English is it – and it will be for my lifetime, I should think.

There is plenty of work here, with lots of schoolchildren, college students and business people keen to learn, either because they have to in order to pass an exam or finish a course or because they need to for work, or sometimes because they just want to learn. I have got most of my pupils through word of mouth and built up a reasonable business and reputation over the last couple of years. I started with two school kids, who were friends of my Spanish tutor's children and whose family were relocating to the USA, and progressed from there. The father of another child who came for lessons worked for a company looking to improve its staff's English, so I was asked to work for them too and my client list has just grown like that.

> **Madrid is a surprisingly cheap city to live in if you don't feel the need to eat in the best places every night and wear designer clothes**

The hourly rate you earn isn't always impressive because there is quite a lot of competition – teaching English is big business in Spain. If you have just one pupil, you might only get six or seven euros an hour, but if you get a group of three or four pupils who come at the same time and charge them five euros each, your hourly rate obviously goes up considerably. And with company groups, I can charge around twenty-five euros per hour, depending on various factors.

That might not sound much if you are used to a New York or London paycheck, but it is okay here because Madrid is a surprisingly cheap city to live in, especially if you share accommodation and bills like I do and don't feel the need to eat in the best places every night and wear designer clothes. I actually really like the simple life I lead in Madrid. In fact, it is a pared down, minimalist existence. All the possessions I have here are clothes, books, toiletries, CDs, a music player and two suitcases. That is traveling and living light. I really like not having any clutter in my life. And moving around a lot as I have over the past few years encourages you to keep culling your things, which is good. I think too many of us have too much stuff and it ties us down. Madrid has turned me into even more of a short-haired hippie.

Love & Labour-Saving

One of the reasons I came away to Europe was to escape from a messy break-up with my girlfriend in Canada. We had been together for five years and were very close so it was difficult. I realize that it is a cliché to run away to escape a failed romance, but it does work, so I recommend it. I didn't meet anybody in London but things have changed in Madrid. I had wondered if Spanish girls would be difficult to meet and get to know, particularly with the language barrier, but people are friendly here and I speak reasonable Spanish now, although I still find it constantly frustrating not being able to express myself as well as I can in English – that takes long years of practice. And humor doesn't always translate. I have got quite a British, absurdist sense of humor, and you have to be careful with that, because it doesn't always transfer easily into another language. But this is the country of Picasso, Dalí, Bunuel and Almodovar, so Spaniards do have a sense of the weird and the absurd.

> *girls like British, American and north European men because they aren't as possessive and controlling as some Spanish men*

At the risk of sounding like a big-headed North American, Spanish girls seem to like me. I suppose it is partly to do with being a foreigner, especially a Canadian, because there aren't too many of us here and I am a novelty. But I have been told by several Spanish and Hispanic girls that they like British, American and north European men because they aren't as possessive and controlling as some Spanish men. I think Spanish men are probably becoming less like that and more international in their approach, but that clinginess is still there, and Spanish women can be the same with their boyfriends and husbands. But some Spanish women find it refreshing to go out with a foreigner. Thank goodness!

I think it might be easier for a foreigner to meet women here in Madrid than in other parts of Spain because there are a lot of sophisticated, internationally-minded people in Madrid, although I am certain that the inhabitants of Barcelona would argue that there are more in their city. I had better be careful about getting into all that, given the rivalry between Madrid and Barcelona.

I have a British passport (I have a lot of family in Scotland) and as an EU 'citizen', I have had little trouble with immigration, etc., although I think the 'no barriers in Europe' publicity is over-egged – it isn't completely straightforward to settle here. But I didn't really have much hassle and because I haven't bought a house or car or set up a complicated business or sued anybody, I have had little experience of the red tape and the pettiness of Spanish civil servants and lawyers, but I have heard that they exist. As for business and tax matters, I employ a professional to deal with all that, so I just let him get on with the complicated hassle, which is by far the best way; don't try to sort it out yourself.

As a general comment, if you speak reasonable Spanish, don't lose your temper and be persistent and patient; you can deal with most encounters with officials and bureaucracy in Spain, but you have to be prepared to queue and also to show a certain amount of self-assertion when dealing with officialdom. As much as possible, however, pay somebody else to do it for you.

Exploring

One of the great things about Madrid is its central position, so nowhere else in Spain is too far away. You can also get a flight to just about anywhere in the world, although long-distance flights are sometimes cheaper via London or Amsterdam. I have traveled around quite extensively in Spain, often at weekends – in the long summer holiday I have usually stayed in Madrid for a week or two to enjoy the late nights and then been to Scotland or back to Canada for the rest of the time.

I really like Galicia in the north-west of Spain. It has beautiful countryside and coastline, and great food and wine. The Basque country is the same and I like the countryside around Madrid too, although hiring a car to drive there can be quite an experience. Spanish drivers are aggressive to say the least and I am not yet comfortable on Spanish roads, although I haven't driven on them too much. I might get used to it with more practice, although some of my foreign friends try to drive as little as possible because it stresses them out too much.

The place that surprised me most in Spain was Benidorm, a holiday resort on the Costa Blanca, halfway down the east coast. From what I had heard about it and seen on TV, I thought I might hate it, but it was great fun. I went there for a long weekend with some Irish friends and really enjoyed myself. I had never been to a resort quite like it before and, although you might not like what it offers, you can't deny that it does it well. And you can speak English everywhere, which was a pleasant change. I shouldn't say that, as a language teacher!

I also want to travel to the Balearics and Canaries, as well as the Moorish cities of the south – Seville, Cordoba and Granada. And I would like to explore more of the Spanish-speaking world. My Argentinean flat mate's stories about his home country have inspired me to go there, but I am going to wait until they sort out their economy.

My experiences of traveling in Spain have been positive. The trains are clean, fast and often inexpensive, although you sometimes have to work hard at fathoming the timetables. And you can get cheap flights between the cities if you shop around and book at the right times. Spain is like a small continent really, with green, wet areas in the north, semi-desert in the south-east, and a lot in between. And having the chance to explore all that is one of the best things about living here.

There are so many good things about living in Madrid. The people, the food, the wines (I have become very keen on Spanish wines), the late nights, the relaxed attitude to most things and all the culture. And I like the fact that the Spanish aren't usually as obsessed with money, career and status as people in London, New York and other big cities. The way you live your life and behave are seen as important here, and everybody is accorded respect, whatever their status in life – accorded respect, that is, unless they do something to lose it. I don't think there are any really bad things about living here, but it does take a long time properly to settle and feel at home in another culture.

I love living here, but I don't actually feel at home yet. It doesn't necessarily feel like the place I will stay for the rest of my days. That is partly because of my decision not to put down any roots. I don't own a home here, or even a car. But I am starting to think about where I want to base myself; I think the same would apply if I was in Paris or Rome. Spain is a very civilized place to live, particularly if you like football, staying up late and missing appointments! And my reservations about staying long-term aren't because I don't like it, but just because I haven't finished traveling and exploring yet, and I might find somewhere I like even better. Buenos Aires? Venice? Sydney?

It's a big world and I reckon most people should try to live in another country for at least a while, preferably one with a different language and culture. And Spain and Madrid are good choices, much better than many. It is best to do it before you have ties like wives, husbands, kids, pets, loans and all the rest. But it can also be easier to meet people as a couple or with kids.

The best way to integrate is to throw yourself into the culture from the start. Get out there and meet people immediately – not just other foreigners. It helps greatly if you speak at least some of the language when you arrive. And the better you learn it, the better your time abroad will be, both in and out of work.

> *most things take longer to arrange*
> *than you might think, which*
> *means that they tend to cost more*
> *than you thought or wanted*

Don't expect the move to be easy. I have had moments when I have thought of leaving, especially when one pupil stopped turning up, owing me money. It wasn't much money – I don't usually give credit and people normally pay up-front – just enough to really piss me off at an already difficult time. And you will feel homesick at times. But remember that this often isn't a bad reflection on the country you are in, so much as a good reflection on the country you have left, which is a positive thing in some ways.

The internet makes it much easier to emigrate than it used to be. It makes keeping in touch with family and friends so much quicker and cheaper than it was. And I recommend that you have family and friends visit you – it helps settling in. I have had people come from Canada and Scotland, which has been great.

You also have to give things time in Spain. Most things take longer to arrange and get organized than you might think, which means that they tend to cost more than you had thought or wanted. But overall, I think most foreigners enjoy their life in Madrid – the ones I know anyway.

A Good Choice

Originally from Twickenham in England, Irene and
Roy Dennis moved from Nigeria to Mijas Costa.
More than 20 years later, Irene is still struggling with
the language – and officialdom.

The reason we came to Spain was a very specific incident, which I remember well. My late husband Roy and I were in England on leave from Africa in June 1978. We were in the garden reading the Sunday papers and Roy spotted an advert for inspection flights to come to see properties in Spain. This was before the recession of the early 1980s when such flights were very common. We liked the sound of it and less than a week later we came out for an inspection weekend.

Everything was beautifully arranged and we immediately had a very good impression of the country. We were met at the airport, taken to where we were dining that night, and the lamb we were to eat was already cooking on a charcoal fire. We ate under the stars and were then taken to the hotel where we were staying. So Spain seemed good to us! Our only previous visit to the country had been a brief trip to Madrid.

Over the next couple of days we were taken to see various building developments, at several spots along the Costa del Sol, and it was one of the last that we were really taken with so we bought it. I still live there now, twenty-six years later, which shows what a good choice we made. We had our first holiday in the apartment in September 1978, but didn't move here full-time until we left Africa and retired, which was in 1983.

Rather Like Africa

We had originally thought of staying in Africa after we retired. But following independence, the situation in many African countries deteriorated, so it didn't seem like a good idea. The part of Nigeria where we were had become incredibly corrupt and the infrastructure was beginning to fall to bits, with power cuts, etc. - the power cuts were actually a good preparation for Spain, because they still happen here too!

> *if you aren't an adaptable sort of person, I don't think there is much point in leaving home*

We had been away from the UK for so long that it felt like abroad, so we didn't really consider retiring there. It still feels foreign when I go back now. When we arrived in Spain for the first time, we noticed similarities with Africa. We were here in June for the inspection tour, so it was hot, like much of Africa, and we also saw a lot of sub-tropical and tropical flowers and trees that we recognised. Spain also has the sort of laid-back feeling you used to have in Africa.

It was probably easier for us than it was for Britons to buy property in Spain in the late 1970s because there were quite severe restrictions on taking money out of the UK back then – I can't remember why. But, because we had been living and working in Nigeria, we brought the money from Africa. It was very different for people from the UK. They had to be devious back then. We heard stories about people bringing the money to buy Spanish properties hidden in their golf bags or even in padded bras!

We found settling into life in Spain easy, but that was because we had long been used to moving around and, besides that, Africa makes you very adaptable. So we didn't have the problems that many people from the UK have had in adapting to life in a new country – it was usual for us. Life in Spain back then was rather different from the way it is now. There was a very restricted amount of consumer goods available, and that must have made the transition for some north Europeans more difficult, not being able to buy what they were used to. I remember that it took me about three weeks to hunt down where I could buy a kettle and, when I found one, it wasn't an electric kettle, but one of those that you put on the top of the stove.

Our transition was easy, but it still took us time to find our feet. I think that a lot of people underestimate the effects of leaving home, family and friends. It is a bit like uprooting a plant: at first, you droop. And it takes quite a long period to adjust – between six months and a year. However adaptable you are, it takes time to find your way around and become familiar with the ways of doing things and so settle. It is the same if you move from one part of England to another, but minus the language barrier. So if you aren't an adaptable sort of person, I don't think there is much point in leaving home.

Don't continually refer to the way things are done in England or wherever it is that you come from. If you do that, to my mind there is only one answer: go back there. You will have to adapt to the way things are done in Spain, including trying to use the language. When I first came here, I needed some information about train travel. With the aid of an English/Spanish Conversation Guide I worded my questions and handed them over at the information desk at the station. The man carefully wrote down the answers, which of course were in Spanish! I thought it was really funny; what else could I expect?

Through Spanish Eyes

The Spanish are generally friendly, open and welcoming people, but I think they have a very mixed view of the foreigners in their country. The yobby types we get down here – mainly British, needless to say – they find totally unacceptable. And I think there are probably some Spaniards who cast us all as being like the bad ones, which is a shame.

But I think that many Spaniards have seen enough of us over a long period of time to realise that we aren't all like the yobs. I hope that continues, but a problem I foresee is that the British who come here now aren't as polite and friendly as they used to be, and people are more suspicious. But let us leave the last word on that subject to the Spanish themselves – British readers might find this a bit depressing.

I recently saw a Spanish-language learning book that the young daughter of a friend was reading and it contained the following two sentences: 'The British like their beer. And they don't like wearing many clothes.' So the image that Spanish people have of the British – that they drink too much and don't know how to dress properly in public – must be very well ingrained in the Spanish mind if it has even made it into children's text books! I hope the football yobs appreciate how bad they make they rest of us look. But of course they don't and, if they did, they wouldn't care.

When we first arrived in Spain we found the red tape difficult, but I am familiar with the way most things work now. It was quite a change from what we were used to, because in Africa the company you work for normally sorts most things out for you. The main problem that you find with officialdom in Spain is that it is almost impossible to get a straight, consistent answer. Different people tell you different things about how to deal with whatever it is – paying your taxes, applying for residence cards and all the rest. In fact, the same person will probably tell you different things at different times!

It can be very frustrating and confusing having to deal with this, but you have to stick to the task and get things done. It is tempting to give up and not see things through, but if you do that, the problem or situation won't go away, and you will only have to sort it out another time. And I think the bureaucracy and red tape in Spain has got better – meaning that it is easier to deal with now. In fact, I think the Spanish have made enormous strides since the 1980s, when things were very basic, primitive even, and disorganised.

But queuing for things is still a way of life here and that looks set to continue. It can be very frustrating because however many people are waiting, the person at the counter will invariably still stop to have a chat if somebody phones or if they are friends with the person at the front of the queue. The thing to do when that happens is to remind yourself of the things that attracted you to Spain in the first place, like its laid-back, sociable way of life, and decide that the person behind the counter is merely being laid-back and sociable.

Another thing I have learned is that it often isn't worth arriving early anywhere where you need to queue, because a lot of Spanish people do the same. There is an idea that the Spanish get up late, but they don't; they get up early, especially if there is queuing to be done, which is quite often.

Communal Living

I generally get on with my neighbours very well, but most of the people on this urbanisation are civilised, and that isn't the case everywhere. I think you have to try to be choosy about where you live, but there is also luck in it. You can't tell who is going to move into a place in the future. The most common problem we have here – as everywhere in this country – is noise. Spain and Italy are the noisiest countries in Europe, and if noisemongers move into the urbanisation it can be a problem.

What a lot of people don't realise is that, when you are living in a community, you have to think about others. You need to conform to the rules. People usually do where I live, although when we have short-term visitors on holiday, they sometimes want to let their hair down too much. I can understand why, because we go on holiday to relax, but it can cause problems for the permanent residents. You only need one rowdy family who don't control their kids at the swimming pool to spoil it for everybody else.

There are also problems living in urbanisations that have residents' committees, which is the law in Spain. A lot of people aren't used to being told what to do with their properties, but there has to be a central ruling body in this country. We find that a lot of people who come to live here are happy to take the benefits that community living gives – having the insurance, decorating, gardening, etc. arranged for you – but they aren't willing to get involved themselves; they don't want to give anything. Too many people just whinge, but aren't prepared to sort anything out themselves. At the annual meetings, the people with the most queries are often the ones who do the least to help. And you can tell that they have been working out what to say for weeks or months before the meeting – sad people!

anything to do with the law in Spain is so complex that I don't think foreigners ever crack how the system works

Another thing is that quite a lot of people who buy property in Spain don't seem to be aware of the community aspect of living here. They might know vaguely that there has to be a committee, but they don't seem to know what it means, or that they have shared financial liabilities towards the properties. You would have thought buying abroad was a big enough thing to take the trouble to investigate what is actually involved!

As for Spanish people, I think they are very good at working together and respecting each other, but then they are more used to communal living than many of the foreigners. And the Spanish seem to find the time to be able to get involved with things. I suppose it comes from the strong bonds of family which they have here. Just go to a Spanish wedding to see what I mean. Everybody is well dressed and well behaved, but they all join in and have a great time. Nobody is drunk or rowdy, and there are no shaved heads or piercings. We can learn from them.

The Worst & The Best

I think the worst thing about living in Spain is having to get involved in anything to do with the law, which is sometimes unavoidable. It probably isn't as bad as it was in the old days, when it was common for lawyers not to turn up for meetings or court hearings, but it is still a long, fraught business. Anything to do with the law in Spain is so complex that I don't think foreigners ever crack how the system works. And everything takes so very long – sometimes decades. It may be better now than it was and there is some comeback against incompetent or corrupt lawyers, which there used not to be, but it is still something you very much want to avoid if possible.

with the great increase in road traffic, we have seen the arrival of one of the things that people used to come here to avoid

There is also a lack of consistency in Spain when you try to get things done. You are often told different things, so there is usually an element of doubt, which is a constant frustration. The best things include the health service, which I can't find fault with. I have found the staff to be very eager to help, polite and thorough, and there is usually an interpreter available to help foreigners. They also offer lots of extra tests and treatments and the local hospital, the Costa del Sol, is excellent. The only drawback at the local clinic is that the queues are getting longer, but then more and more people are coming to live here and using the services.

We also have a nice climate to live in and a sociable way of life, and I like the fact that where we live is on a hill so it hasn't been possible to surround it with high-rise developments, which has happened in too many places. So we still enjoy great views of the sea on one side and the mountains on the other.

And last but not least, my friend Betty mentioned that she likes the fact that the funerals are very well organised here! But you have got to think about these things as you get older. They are very sensitive about funerals in Spain and they will adapt them to how you want the service, which is great. And they don't hang around – funerals happen very quickly after a death, which is much better than in the UK, where the bereaved have to hang around for a week or ten days, which is torture, because nobody can settle and grieve.

My husband died here in 1990, but in spite of all the problems you read about in UK funeral director advertising aimed at expats living in Spain, I didn't experience problems. If you have Spanish friends, which you should have when you live in Spain, they will guide you in the right direction. And I continue to enjoy life here in Spain even though I am alone.

As for changes I have seen, there is a much greater foreign presence and influence in Spain now than when we arrived. It is much more international than it used to be. Unfortunately, with the great increase in the amount of road traffic, we have seen the arrival of one of the things that people used to come here to avoid. And other bad things have arrived here recently too, like graffiti and the keying of cars, but I wonder if they have been copied from foreigners. Spanish children generally don't seem to be quite as polite and well behaved as they used to be.

But not all the changes I have seen have been bad. There are so many more facilities here for foreigners than there used to be. We have plenty of supermarkets and cinemas now, whereas we used to have to go all the way to Puerto Banus to see a film. In fact, there is a great deal more of everything now, thanks to all the building that has gone on, but I wonder if we might soon see the bubble burst.

Retiring To Spain

I think people considering retirement here should do a lot of research before they come out, especially concerning how much it costs to live, including emergency provisions. Make sure you will have enough to live on, not just now but in the future. And don't imagine you will get any state handouts in Spain.

Choose where you live carefully, because age is a factor in deciding where to live. You might fancy a country retreat or a mountain-top villa, but it isn't very practical if you need ready access to medical services or other help. And you will have an easier and better social life if you live on an urbanisation or in town. You also need to look at things like public transport. We have a good local bus service, which makes the journey into town easy and cheap, but a lot of places haven't. And you need to think about whether you want to run a car and whether you are suited to driving in Spain, which isn't always the most restful place to take to the roads.

I also think that older people living in Spain need to be prepared to help themselves and not expect everything to be done for them and brought to them.

*there are also plenty of clubs
and organisations to get
involved with . . . but you have to
get out there and join in*

Get to know the systems here and the ways things work. The language can be a big hurdle, of course. There are plenty of us who have been here for twenty or twenty-five years and speak little of it. The British seem to be the worst of the foreigners for that. You also have to be prepared to stick at things if you want to live in Spain. Too many older people here don't seem to want to do anything for themselves and think that people owe them something just because they are old.

Make use of the many organisations in Spain which are there to help. Our Town Hall runs a very good Foreigners' Department, which dispenses all sorts of advice and help, and the local Tourist Offices are usually good too. That sort of thing has improved a lot in recent years and people should take advantage of it. There are also plenty of clubs and organisations to get involved with, including branches of the British Legion, bridge clubs, bowls clubs and lots more. But you have to get out there and join in.

Best Of Both Worlds

Born in Exeter, England, Tony Matthews took early retirement and moved to Sotogrande on the Costa del Sol with his wife. They were soon disillusioned with the 'sunny coast' and hankered after . . . Bristol.

There were a few reasons behind our decision to come to Spain. I had had a stressful job and retired early because of high blood pressure and a minor heart problem, so we were looking for a relaxed pace of life to nurse me back to health. My father had lived to be eighty-seven and I wanted to copy him. We thought Spain was a good choice as a laid-back location, we had enjoyed holidays here and I play some golf – Spain has plenty of courses. We also thought that it would be a nice climate to live in. Sarah used to get depressed in the English winter and the doctor mentioned SAD (seasonal affective disorder). People who get it become depressed by a lack of sunlight.

As well as these reasons, we thought it was time to leave Britain. It had become very crowded, crime was on the rise and we saw things getting worse rather than better. Even with these gripes, however, we kept a flat in Bristol, which we went back to regularly to see family and friends. We no longer live in Spain full-time, spending some of the year in the Bristol flat.

Two New Ways Of Life

We found settling into life in Spain straightforward. We had bought a villa shortly before I retired and moved out almost immediately after my last day at work. So it was like two whole new ways of life at the same time: no work and a new country to live in. The relief at no longer working made us both happy and relaxed and that helped us to settle into the new country. We came out in June, which is one of the nicest months, and the first three or four months was like a long holiday. We had a lot of family and friends out to stay during that period, which helped us to settle because it meant we didn't miss people too much.

> **Spain simply isn't geared up for heavy rain: you get landslips, roads subside and the drains back up and burst**

I put on a lot of weight quite quickly, however. Because those first months saw so many family members and friends coming out, I did a lot of sitting around the pool and eating and drinking too much. It was lovely but bad for the old ticker. I lost the weight in the autumn when I started to play golf and went on the Atkins diet, which definitely works. From what I have read, it might not be great for the health long term, but it certainly shifts the old pounds.

We enjoyed the first autumn in Spain and began to make some friends locally, mainly other Brits, but then got a bit of a shock the first winter. The thing that tripped us up was the thing that most people come out here for: the weather. It just rained and rained, for weeks at a time. I seem to remember that in the January, which was probably the worst month, that it rained just about every day. And I am not talking about just a few showers, but hard rain for hours and hours on end.

For a start, bad weather takes away Spain's main attraction for lots of us sun-starved folk, but it is worse than that. Spain simply isn't geared up for heavy rain. You get landslips, roads subside and the drains back up and burst. The electricity also goes off because the wires are often laid overground and aren't properly insulated, so they get wet. How primitive is that? But worst of all, our house turned mouldy.

It was so damp for so long that thick mould grew on parts of most of the walls and ceilings. We had to paint if off every few days with watered-down bleach. The villa didn't have a damp course, like many buildings here; it isn't an uncommon problem. Poor old Sarah: as well as going potty with the bleak weather, she was having to live in a mouldy house that smelled of bleach for about three months.

We also found out the hard way that villas aren't designed for cool weather. They are great in the summer and keep out the heat very efficiently, but in the winter they are like fridges. Our place was open plan with marble floors and we would huddle in the living area wearing several layers of sweaters – gloves sometimes – like a couple of refugees. Even with plenty of gas heaters, which we rushed out to buy, it never really got warm because there weren't any doors to keep the heat in. We ended up spending most of our time in the small study, which did have a door and could be warmed up properly. But we hadn't moved to Spain to live like a pair of students.

The Rain In Spain . . .

So lesson one that we learned was that Spain's weather isn't as good as we had thought. Between October and April it can be quite rough, especially down our end of the coast. It is much wetter at the Gibraltar end of the Costa del Sol and gets warmer, drier and sunnier as you go east; Almeria has the best weather on the mainland of Spain. Where we live now, on the Costa Blanca, seems to be quite a lot drier than Sotogrande.

We thought that the first winter on the Costa del Sol might be a one-off and that others would be better, but they were wet too. There had been several years of drought prior to 1995, and the lack of water was becoming grave, but then the dry period ended and the weather seemed to enter a 'wetter winter' phase. It is probably just global climate change, but when the climate deteriorates in a holiday region it is a particular problem, especially for a region that sells itself on year-round sun – even names itself after it. And you don't get that on the Costa del Sol any more. I think a lot of people noticed it in 1997, when they held the Ryder Cup at Valderrama, which is near Sotogrande. It rained almost continually – and it was in September, which is meant to be one of the best weather months. I wonder how many potential holidaymakers that put off coming.

I am not saying that the Costa del Sol's winter weather isn't better than the UK's. It is, but the UK's is pretty awful. When it is nice in the winter in Spain, it is lovely, but it isn't nice often enough for my liking and it is unpredictable. The Costa del Sol has just had the wettest autumn for sixty years and the wettest spring for around forty, so it isn't settling down. And I have recently found out that it used to be called the Costa del Viento, the windy coast. But it was renamed the Costa del Sol, the sunny coast, by government officials who wanted to boost tourist numbers and thought there would be more sunseekers than windsurfers – a clever ruse.

As the old name suggests, the coast can get very windy, although not as windy as the area around Tarifa and the Costa de la Luz on the way to the Algarve. It is so windy on the beaches there that, if you don't find adequate shelter, you end up getting sand-blasted. If you want the best weather and pretty much guaranteed winter sun and warmth, don't live in mainland Spain, but go to the Canaries. They have much better weather: warmer and drier in the winter, and fresher in the summer.

In fact, I think that the Costa del Sol needs to develop other attractions to draw visitors. As well as the weather becoming unpredictable, not so many people want sun and beach holidays any more. So the tourist authorities need to offer different things, and I think they have now realised that. Fuengirola has recently revamped its zoo – and very well too. And the new Picasso Museum in Malaga has been a great success, with queues to get in on many days. They need more attractions like those.

Comparing Costas

As well as for the seemingly better weather (I don't want to tempt fate) we moved to the Costa Blanca because the Costa del Sol was beginning to turn into a building site, even at our less developed end of the coast. I haven't been back recently, but I understand from friends that the building has got even worse. I have heard that within ten years, the entire coast from Gibraltar to Nerja and maybe beyond will be completely built up, making it the largest unbroken strip of building development in Europe. It sounds like a nightmare and I can't understand why the authorities don't see the damage they are doing. The short-term gain will be wiped out if they ruin their coast for the long term and I think they should impose a year-long suspension of all new building while they decide on some type of development policy.

We also found airport access was difficult living in Sotogrande. Gibraltar airport is much nearer than Malaga's, but the queues to get in and out of Gibraltar can be horrendous. The Spanish authorities deliberately make it hard and slow to get in and out, which is a childish protest against the Rock being British. So it makes getting in and out of Gibraltar uncertain and stressful, which is no good when you are trying to catch a flight and have a dodgy heart!

Malaga airport isn't much better because it is a long drive from Sotogrande, even on a clear road, which the N-340 motorway never is. I think it is the worst road I have driven on – joint first with the M25. We found using the N-340 very stressful. The volume of traffic is huge and the accident rate is horrendous, as are the delays when there is an accident. There is a new motorway now, inland of the N-340, which is meant to be good, but you have to pay, which I object to. So I wouldn't recommend that anybody who flies a lot and needs an easy journey to an airport lives on the far western Costa del Sol.

> *we had thought it might be more 'chicken and chips, ten pints of lager and a fight' than parts of the Costa del Sol*

We thought of moving to the Canaries for the weather and went out there in 1998 to explore. But we didn't really like the two islands we went to, Tenerife and Lanzarote, which were either too built up or too underdeveloped. The weather was mixed too: Tenerife was cloudy and Lanzarote was very windy. And we found them expensive, and just that bit too far from the UK for easy hops back.

So we visited friends on the Costa Blanca and loved it. We had thought it might be more 'chicken and chips, ten pints of lager and a fight' than parts of the Costa del Sol, but we were pleasantly surprised. It has its black spots but overall it is more unspoiled, especially the north of the Costa. And it is cheaper, by about a third.

It is also more peaceful here, the travel links are better and I think the winter weather is more settled than in Sotogrande. Our one quibble is the summers, which are hotter. Sotogrande has great summers, rarely too warm, but it can be steaming here from mid-June into October. But we are usually back in Bristol then. And we bought a smaller place here than we had in Sotogrande, with doors rather than open plan, which is much easier to heat in the winter. It gets more winter sun than the place in Sotogrande used to, and sun dries the walls out, so we don't have anything like the same damp problem, although we do get the odd patch, so the smell of bleach still sometimes makes my nose burn!

The Good, The Bad & The Inefficiency

We have found making friends easy in Spain, but we are quite sociable people. I used to be in sales, which was all about people, and Sarah is the same – a people person. One of the good things about the expatriate community here is the variety. We like living with people from lots of different countries, although most of our friends are either British or Scandinavian. The 'Scandies' tend to speak good English, which helps.

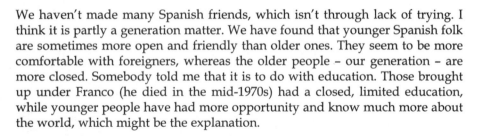

> *it takes a long, long time to become fluent. I don't think I will live long enough to get there*

We haven't made many Spanish friends, which isn't through lack of trying. I think it is partly a generation matter. We have found that younger Spanish folk are sometimes more open and friendly than older ones. They seem to be more comfortable with foreigners, whereas the older people – our generation – are more closed. Somebody told me that it is to do with education. Those brought up under Franco (he died in the mid-1970s) had a closed, limited education, while younger people have had more opportunity and know much more about the world, which might be the explanation.

The Spanish friends we do have are younger, professional people – a doctor and a couple of engineers. We try to speak Spanish, which helps. We are quite good, although it takes a long, long time to become fluent. I don't think I will live long enough to get there.

I think it is maybe easier for older foreigners to make friends in Spain than it is for younger ones. A couple of youthful Brits here have told us that because young people come and go with great frequency, they find it quite difficult to maintain friendships for long. But I think the same problem exists for young people who live in big cities like London - young people are more mobile everywhere now, which means that keeping in touch with friends is hard.

The weather in Spain between the autumn and the spring is generally better than in the UK and this has a beneficial psychological effect, especially on people, like Sarah, with SAD. It also has a big influence on how you are able to live life. A lot more time can be spent outdoors, meaning that life is more active, sporty and sociable. We often eat lunch outdoors, on a sheltered terrace, even in the middle of winter, unless it is raining.

I stressed the better weather in Spain between autumn and spring because I actually think that the weather in southern England is better between May or June and September or October than it is here. Summers in England are definitely longer and warmer than they used to be. And it gets very hot here in the summer – too hot really. It is fine for a two- or three-week holiday, but if you spend a whole summer here it gets very tiring. And I say that as a retired person who doesn't have to go out and about. I don't know how people who have to work cope with the heat.

We read a report by some American scientists which predicted that the south-east of Spain would become an extension of the Sahara within twenty or thirty years, as part of global warming. So a future version of this book might say that the worst aspect of living on the Costa Blanca is that it is too hot for habitation for three or four months a year. I can't imagine how that would damage the tourist business.

Another positive thing about living here is being able to get to know Spain. And there is a lot to know. We have been to wildly different places. Galicia in the north-west looks like a cross between Ireland and Norway. It is green and wet like Ireland and has fjords like Norway. We have also visited Almeria province, which is the complete opposite, with stretches of semi-desert. They filmed some of those Clint Eastwood spaghetti westerns there in the 1960s and you can visit cowboy-style film sets. So there is a wide range of scenery and attractions. We like Spain's cities too. It is a great country for just packing a weekend bag and heading off in the car for a few days or a week, as the fancy takes you, and seeing where you end up. That is a definite advantage of living here.

We also enjoy Spanish food and wines, and have become keen gardeners, which we never were in England. You can grow fruit and vegetables all year round in much of Spain, which is great. As for the golf, I don't play as much as I used to because it is becoming more expensive; course owners are getting greedy, I'm afraid, as happened on the Costa del Sol.

The worst aspects of life in Spain are probably the disorganisation and inefficiency. You often seem to have to battle to get things done, certainly anything involving officialdom, banks and taxes. Having a laid-back approach to life is good in some ways, but you don't want to become so laid-back that you never get anything done properly. I also worry that the Costa Blanca will become as overbuilt as the Costa del Sol within a decade or so. And last, but not least, two petty problems about living in Spain: as a big chap, I have trouble getting shoes and clothes that fit me, and flamenco music blaring out of cars and bars drives me potty - I can't stand it!

Tied To The Old Country

I am not sure whether to recommend retirement to Spain or not. It depends so much on the individual – or individuals if you are a couple. It suits some people down to the ground, but others begin to hate it after the first few months or so. We have seen plenty of examples of both. So I would suggest that people do a lot more research about a possible move than we did. We jumped in a bit and bought the wrong type of property in the wrong place. We were lucky that we were able to sell it easily, but the market is flat at the moment, so anyone in a similar situation might be stuck where they are, unless they were prepared to sell at a loss.

We have also found it to be a lot more expensive to live here than we had thought it would be, especially over the last couple of years. It was cheap when we first arrived but it isn't now, so if you are on a modest pension you might struggle. We have seen quite a lot of other retirees who scrimp to make ends meet.

I also think that some folks who move to Spain underestimate the amount that they will miss family and friends at home. When we first came out, we had a lot of visitors from Britain, which was great. But over time, some of those people have come out to visit us less and less. That isn't because we have fallen out or anything, but simply because there are so many places to take your holidays other than Spain. And we know of retirees here who have missed their grandchildren so much that they have gone back to the UK, feeling that by living in Spain they are missing them growing up. We also know of one couple whose kids are pressuring them to return to Wales because they want them to help with the grandchildren, who have gone off the rails a bit. They can't cope with their own kids, so they want the grandparents to throw in the towel in Spain and go back to save the day!

I would also advise people to give it a decent go before deciding whether life in Spain suits them or not. That probably means moving around a few times to see what type of area and property suits you. You are unlikely to find the ideal the first time. And rent before you buy, both in winter and summer, to see what it is like in the different seasons. Some folk prefer the winter, others like the heat.

I am not sure that I would recommend a move to Spain for younger people who need to work, unless they are working for a foreign firm at foreign wage levels. Of the young foreigners we know here, most seem to work hard for pretty modest rewards. Some of them make decent money, but they seem to be the exception, and one of the most common complaints among working expatriates is that the money is poor.

> *I don't think people realise*
> *what a great place Britain*
> *actually is and how much it*
> *has to offer until they leave it*

When we first arrived in Spain, earning lower wages wasn't so much of a problem because the cost of living was low too, but it isn't any more. You can have a great life here if you've got money, but not such a good one if you haven't. We know a family who loved the life here, particularly for their kids, but they had to go back to the UK because they couldn't make enough money in Spain, or rather not make enough money consistently enough. And the inconsistency of what they earn seems to be a growing problem for people who work in industries directly connected with tourist customers, because there has been a dip in tourist numbers at certain times of the year. I don't think the Madrid bomb helped tourist confidence. And exotic holidays are much cheaper than they used to be, so people are going further afield. But most of all, I think the problem is that people who want a beach holiday have probably decided that they have 'done' Spain and are looking to go to Turkey, Cyprus or Portugal.

Overall, I think I have come to the conclusion that the British aren't really suited to living abroad full time. The ideal scenario for retired British people is to live here part of the year, and spend the rest of the time in Britain. And I don't mean that as a bad reflection on Spain, but as a good one on Britain. I don't think people realise what a great place Britain actually is and how much it has to offer until they leave it. And it is definitely true that we usually try to remake Britain wherever we live. You saw it during the time of our empire, when a quarter of the world was pink and we recreated a little Britain everywhere from India to Kenya to Canada. That probably shows more than anything how attached we are to the old country.

A Perfect Retirement

Christine and Ron Goodwin, originally from Kent
in England, retired to Mijas and have never looked
back – despite the builders, the bureaucracy,
the drivers and the drug-takers . . .

W e bought a holiday apartment here way back in 1978, so we had been to the country numerous times before we came out here permanently and knew the area and plenty of people, so it was a sort of natural progression. We had come to love the country and the climate over the years of visiting and, when we took early retirement – on 16th December 1995 to be exact – we came out immediately. In fact, a day later, on the 17th December, we were sitting on our suitcases waiting for the train at Malaga airport in fresh air and brilliant sunshine. And it felt very comfortable for us, right from the start. We knew we had made the correct decision to retire here and still feel the same nearly ten years later.

The Way It Was

The country was so much less developed when we first came, in 1978. There was no public transport from our urbanisation to town, for example, so we used to walk everywhere. Then the local council provided a bus service, but it was unlike any bus we had ever used before because when it rained the roof of the bus became a sieve and water flooded in! You had to check the seats as you went past to see which, if any, were dry, before deciding where or whether to sit down.

Somebody then took the initiative and tried to fill the holes in the roof, with blobs of chewing gum. The driver also became sick of getting wet and fitted the upper part of an umbrella over his seat! On one occasion, a little old lady vociferously berated him and insisted that she wasn't going to pay her fare to sit on a wet seat. Everything is much slicker and more modern now, which is good in some ways, but it isn't as characterful and quirky as it was.

And the pace of life is much faster now – more international. We know of people who think the Spanish have become more arrogant as they have become wealthier. And they certainly have a lot more money than when we arrived. You can see it in the number and quality of cars on the roads. Back in the 1970s they were few and far between, and the ones you did come across were usually battered and rickety.

The sleepy, laid-back Spain of old has definitely gone, certainly on this coast. Nobody spoke English when we first started coming, but people still managed to be friendly and tolerant. The locals are still patient and tolerant with most foreigners today, but probably not as much as they used to be. Another big change is the amount of property development; there is so much building now. It seems to be relentless and I think it has made some parts of the coast feel overdone.

Getting By

I think the only way to learn the language properly is to integrate with the Spanish people. You can only get so far with lessons. We have heard that the very best way to learn is to live with a Spanish family and immerse yourself in the language, because ideally you have to practise all the time. But you should wait until you have reached at least a reasonable level of Spanish and can build from there. It also apparently helps if there is an English-speaker in the family, to explain things to you when needed.

> *the red tape and bureaucracy in Spain can be a nightmare and are definitely one of the worst aspects of living in this country*

We have found that going away on pensioners' trips with other Spanish people is beneficial for our language skills. We are forced to use our Spanish all the time because a lot of them don't have even a word of English. In fact, quite a lot of Spanish people don't and we foreigners can get into trouble when we try to speak their language. A friend of ours decided to get a haircut in the local Spanish barbershop and thought his Spanish was good enough to request 'just a trim all over'. But he emerged from the chair with very little hair left, resembling a hedgehog or a toilet brush, because the barber thought he had wanted 'just a little left all over'. He had about 2mm of hair remaining, when he had been hoping to fashion his trimmed hair into a style with a ponytail, he joked. At least he didn't have to have another haircut for six months, but he headed straight back to Spanish classes to improve his language skills.

The red tape and bureaucracy in Spain can be a nightmare and are definitely one of the worst aspects of living in this country. Unlike some people who come to live here, we have done everything officially, and applied for Spanish residence, a social security card, pensioners' card, local driving licence, etc., and it has been something of a trial getting it all done. It is apparently much easier – although costly – to use a *gestor* or a solicitor, but we decided to do it ourselves in order to find out how everything works – or rather doesn't work.

We have found that the worst department to deal with is Traffic. We once exchanged UK for Spanish driving licences. Nothing could be more straightforward in theory, but you have to queue for a ticket, queue to pay, then queue again at *Conductores* to actually exchange the licences. In fact, it took us four separate trips to Malaga to finalise the matter, although it was complicated by the fact that my licence was stolen between visits, which added another layer of red tape to the whole thing.

But we have tried to view dealing with the bureaucracy in Spain as an experience rather than a nightmare and you will have a more relaxed time here if you try to do the same. There is no point in becoming hassled and hot under the collar because it just makes everything more difficult and people less responsive.

We have found the health system to be excellent. Our local hospital – called the Costa del Sol hospital – is in Marbella. It has only two patients to a room, and each room has an en suite bathroom, TV and telephone. The phone only takes incoming calls, unless you buy tokens, which allow you to make outward calls and also to watch TV in your own language. There are also quite a number of interpreters available and some of the staff speak some English. We cannot speak highly enough of the treatment and follow-up examinations, and understand that other Spanish hospitals offer similar levels of care, which is a great reflection on the country's health service.

Joining In

Our leisure is pretty different here. In the UK we used to enjoy gardening and indoor bowls. We also ate out occasionally and spent time shopping, usually at large indoor shopping centres. The climate in southern Spain means that you can do a lot more things outdoors, for much of the year. We play tennis, swim, go bowling and eat out or go to bars a lot more, because it is much cheaper than in the UK, although not as cheap as it used to be.

you have to make the effort to break the ice but, if you do, you can have a really good time

We also go on a fair number of trips within Spain, some of which are organised for local pensioners by the Town Hall. Some of these trips are free, some attract a nominal charge. There are often few Brits on them, so we are something of a novelty. We went to Almeria and Mojacar a few months ago, and there were a mere eight foreigners out of a total of 650 travellers. We have found that Spanish pensioners are a bit reticent with us at first but, when you get over that, they are very friendly and welcoming and go out of their way to include us in everything. You have to make the effort to break the ice – you are the outsider after all – but, if you do, you can have a really good time. I just wish more foreigners would make that effort.

Overall, I think there is a lot more available to retired people here than there is in England. People get out and about so much more and socialise. And it is reckoned to put years on your lifespan. We have also found that close friends seem to be closer here than back in the UK and make up for the lack of family. Even acquaintances seem to be more friendly. In general, the Spanish are very tolerant and easy to approach, especially if you make an effort to communicate and join in their activities, which we do. We have made friends with people from the pensioners' trips that we mentioned earlier and have also become close to some of our Spanish neighbours, particularly one young couple with children. They have moved a short distance away now to a bigger house, but we regularly go to stay with them.

The more sociable lifestyle here makes it easier to meet new people, but it must be said that they aren't always the type you want to meet. The expatriate community can be a bit claustrophobic, particularly the people in all-British urbanisations, restaurants, bars and social clubs. We try to avoid the types of Brits who just want to recreate the home country in the sun and also the dodgy ones who would rip anybody off.

And I think that the Spanish sometimes have a problem with what they see as bad behaviour, either by their own people or foreigners. You don't have to spend long here to see foreigners drinking too much, getting rowdy, etc. But overall I think they are very tolerant of us, more than they sometimes appear. The Spanish can come across as more disapproving and confrontational than they actually are. They often shout when they speak and make dramatic gestures, which gives the impression of aggression when none is meant. It is just a different way of approaching things – a cultural difference.

Community Life

We have had quite a lot of building work done, both to the apartment we own as well as to the house we now live in. One thing we have noticed about Spanish builders is that they tend to try to tell you what you want done, rather than asking you what you want done. What they are actually doing is telling you the work that they want to do, which is interesting! And I know that other people have had the same experience as us, so they aren't isolated incidents.

We have found that the standard of work done is generally good or very good, although not always so, but you do have to keep a regular eye on the work as it proceeds. If things are done wrong, rather than trying to solve the problem, the builder is highly likely to try to convince you that there isn't a problem, and will even get touchy if you disagree with him. For example, one Spanish builder who did some work on our apartment kitchen put an electric power socket right above the gas rings, making it unusable when cooking. When we pointed this out, he said, "No problem; only use it when you aren't cooking."

Our entire urbanisation is the best example we have heard about of the importance of keeping an eye on builders. Believe it or not, it is strongly rumoured that they built the apartments where the townhouses should have been, and vice versa. It seems incredible that nobody noticed such a huge mistake when the land was being marked out, but it makes sense that they got it wrong because the cheaper apartments have much better sea and mountain views than the more expensive townhouses, and it is invariably the other way round: the better properties are built with the better views.

There is also the *mañana* attitude to contend with, although that seems to apply to builders everywhere. So we recommend that you tell your builders the deadline is at least three weeks before you actually need the work done. And don't forget that things take longer here in the summer, or work might stop altogether – particularly in August, which is the holiday month.

All Spanish apartment blocks or urbanisations (housing and apartment developments) have, by law, to have a committee, to deal with communal matters and facilities, e.g. electricity, water, exterior painting and maintenance, and gardening. A committee is elected from the residents, including a president, who oversees its business and is the ultimate power.

This type of communal living and decision-making is quite alien to most foreigners and can be a shock to the system, especially to Brits who had previously thought that their home was their castle. It might not be in Spain! Ron is on our committee, so he sees what goes on. The amount of whingeing and stupid questions he has to put up with is remarkable.

The problem with the system is that a residents' committee has to try to keep dozens or even hundreds of people happy, which of course involves trying to reach some form of consensus. This, unfortunately, means that quite often things get hopelessly watered down and so nothing really gets done. It is also often the case that different urbanisations don't really work together, even though neighbouring ones are affected by the same things, e.g. problems with local amenities and roads. In fact, they are quite often at loggerheads with each other.

The president of a committee legally has the power to act, for example to collect outstanding community fees or make people take down illegal building work, but they often have to go to court to get anything done, which takes time, trouble and money.

Committees, of course, can encourage self-importance, so you also have to deal with egos and petty politics, which can be time-consuming and tedious. So it is little surprise that so many people don't want to serve on the committees, especially as president. It is a lot of work and often a thankless task, for little if any reward. Some presidents are paid, but many aren't. Ours has her community fees and her telephone bill paid, and we are lucky to have her. She is Danish and puts in a lot of work to keep the community running efficiently and cost-effectively. A good president is a real asset to a community and it is an idea to check out the president before deciding whether to buy in an area. Not, of course, that you can tell how long they will do the job, and the next one might be a nightmare!

One of the more common problems in Spanish urbanisations is with dogs – or rather with owners who let their dogs bark at unsocial times and foul the paths and communal gardens. More and more urbanisations seem to be bringing in rules banning pets, so watch for that if you are an animal lover. Unruly children are also a common problem, especially in places with a lot of retirees who are after a quiet life. Our communal gardens seem to be a gathering ground for noisy teenagers on scooters who get up to who knows what late at night. The gardener finds the evidence the next morning, including used condoms and signs of drug-taking.

> *there are some lovely,
> rolling green hills next to our
> house, which are apparently
> slated for development*

But community living has its benefits. It allows urbanisations to share costs and enjoy facilities that a property on its own couldn't afford. As well as the extensive gardens, which are beautifully maintained by our gardener, we also have access to a swimming pool and tennis court.

Retirement Home

We are generally very happy and believe that life in Spain has surpassed our expectations. We have some grumbles, of course, because nowhere is perfect. The scooters are a menace on the roads, weaving in and out of traffic, often in the blind spot of a car mirror. They are often driven by kids (you can ride one at fourteen, which seems ridiculous, although I have heard that they are going to change the law to increase that to sixteen) and they make a dreadful racket, particularly late at night in the summer, when local youngsters keep very late hours.

We also wonder about the ever-increasing amount of new building and seeming lack of regard for the environment. There are some lovely, rolling green hills next to our house, which are apparently slated for development. It is meant to be low-rise, but we'll see. And the noise and dust while they work is usually very intrusive.

The standard of driving in Spain is generally poor. Spanish drivers don't signal very often and don't like to give way to others. You really need to keep your wits about you when driving here and certainly isn't relaxing, which is a pity. At least the heavy volume of traffic means that people often can't drive too fast, which they seem to like to do when they get the chance. Pedestrians need to be careful when crossing roads, even at crossings, because drivers really don't like to stop.

> *we love the sociable lifestyle,*
> *although it can tempt you to go*
> *out too much and spend more of*
> *your pension than you expect*

In fact, the standard of driving is so low that I would like to know the number of drivers who have actually got licences. A report from four or five years ago estimated that at least twenty-five per cent of Spanish drivers didn't have insurance. Expatriate drivers are a problem too. As well as drinking too much, a lot of foreigners who bring cars here from abroad fail to get them tested regularly, if at all, which means that the insurance is invalidated. In fact, I would recommend that people leave their cars in the home country and buy one here. It is a bureaucratic nightmare trying to make a foreign car legal in Spain, which means a lot of people give up. And driving a British car here is dangerous, because the steering wheel is on the wrong side, so you have restricted vision – a particular problem when trying to pull onto a Spanish motorway, which is dangerous enough anyway.

If you are thinking about coming to try life in Spain, rent a property before committing yourself to a purchase. It is the only way properly to get to know an area, your neighbours, the different seasons and whether it actually suits you to live in Spain. The quality of life here is very good for us retirees, although I am not so sure about younger people who have to work; they almost always seem to have to take a drastic drop in salary from that in their original country. And they work long hours.

We love the sociable lifestyle here, although it can tempt you to go out too much and spend more of your pension than you might expect, which people need to be aware of. As for the Costa del Sol, we have travelled quite extensively in Spain, and haven't found anywhere as good. So we would recommend that other people try the life here. But we do mean 'try' it first. Don't just sell up and come out on a whim. It isn't for everybody.

Different From Denmark

Jeanett Lorentzen moved from Denmark to the
Costa del Sol, having previously lived briefly in Bierzo
in north-west Spain. As a blonde businesswoman in a
dark-haired male-dominated world, she sometimes
finds life in Spain hard work.

There is a long story behind my coming to Spain and getting into the wine business. My dad died when I was seventeen and my mum didn't want to stay in Denmark after that so she came to live in Spain in 1983. I remained in Ålborg, Denmark to finish my education and then I began work, first in a bank and then in real estate. My mum subsequently met the man who has become her second husband, Fernando (who is originally from Tenerife, although he lived in Germany for seventeen years), and he worked in the restaurant business. Through doing that, he had got to know the owner of a wine producer called Palacio de Arganza, based in the wine region of Bierzo in north-west Spain.

My mum knew that I wanted to travel (working in a bank and estate agent's were both a bit plodding and it was going to take too long for me to get anywhere in those conservative sectors) and Fernando found out that the boss of Palacio de Arganza was looking for an assistant to help him with the business, particularly the sales trips abroad – someone who spoke foreign languages [Jeanett speaks six languages fluently: Danish, Swedish, Norwegian, German, Spanish and English] – and they thought of me. So I came to Spain in 1989 and began to work for Palacio de Arganza in Bierzo.

The Wine Trail

I worked mainly on exports and was the right-hand 'man' to the owner, as well as his translator because he only spoke Spanish. I did the job for eight months but decided to give it up because it became really monotonous living out of a suitcase for much of the time, on our sales trips, which were mainly around Germany, Denmark, Sweden and the rest of Spain. It is almost impossible to make, let alone keep, new friends when you are living like that. And when I was in Bierzo, I didn't know anybody and used to spend too much time on my own. It was a very beautiful place, but very cold in the winter.

*they took a bit longer than
some builders would have done,
but the work was done correctly
and all the walls are straight*

After eight months I resigned and decided to go to spend a couple of months with my mum while I decided what to do with my life and career. That is how I arrived on the Costa del Sol, in the early summer of 1990, and I have been here ever since. As well as working in the restaurant business, Fernando had begun to sell wine – Palacio de Arganza's wines. As for me, in addition to working for a firm that distributed Danish products to restaurants, shops and bars along the coast, I also began to help Fernando with the wine sales in my spare time. It was very useful working for the Danish distributor because it meant I got to know the area properly and also began to understand the ways of doing business in this part of the world.

Shortly afterwards, I received an inheritance from my dad and decided to start my own business, Birdie Vinos, along with Fernando. We started small, by selling to restaurants, and then got modest premises in Fuengirola and took it from there. I think we had about three premises there, and then, around four years ago, took the plunge to purpose-build our current building, which is between Fuengirola and Mijas. A year earlier, my partner Ivano (who was originally in the restaurant business – we met at the Seville Expo in 1992) and I had bought Fernando out, when he wanted to retire.

It took around two and a half years from buying the land to actually opening the premises. Getting the permit to build took around six months, but we weren't in a hurry, so it wasn't a problem. And we chose to use builders who had built a villa for my mother so we knew that they were reliable and did a good job, which certainly isn't always the case. They took a bit longer than some builders would have done, but the work was done correctly and all the walls are straight, which is nice! I also had a good architect, which helps.

When I first arrived, integration into life in Spain was easy for me in some ways, but difficult in others. I think that the fact that I spoke reasonable Spanish helped a lot. When my mum decided to move here back in 1983, I thought that it would be a good idea to take Spanish at school, so I had studied it properly before coming here. And when I found out about the job with Palacio de Arganza, I took an intensive Spanish course in Denmark to really improve my skills, which the wine maker kindly paid for. It was me on my own with a tutor, for three hours a day, every day for three weeks; you really learn a lot by studying like that. And speaking the language reasonably well makes a huge difference to whether you integrate or not. Having some of my family living here also made it easier to settle in.

Nevertheless, there are some aspects of life in Spain that I still find difficult to get used to, even after living here all these years. Like a lot of Danes, I am an organised person and I like things to run efficiently, but that doesn't usually happen here, which is frustrating. When we were designing and building the current premises, for example, I wanted to be involved in every little detail, down to the light switches, door handles, everything. But in Spain, with its laid-back attitude, slow pace and sometimes disorganisation, that proved to be a real test of my mental strength and persistence. But you need persistence to get things done here – certainly in the way that you want them done.

I am also quite impatient, so the *mañana* attitude sometimes drives me potty, as does the need to queue for so many things, certainly anything to do with official paperwork. You can queue for ages and when you reach the head of the queue, you find out that you are actually in the wrong queue, or haven't got the right bits of paper with you, so you have to start all over again. I am not sure I will ever get used to that aspect of living here.

Machismo

It can be extremely difficult to be a woman in business, both here and in other parts of Spain. In fact, there are still things that I as a woman cannot get done, not because I am incompetent or inexperienced but simply because of my sex. Either obstacles are put in the way or certain people just aren't prepared to deal with me. When I was in business with Fernando, he had to do certain things, just because he is a man, and likewise now with Ivano. A man simply has to do some things.

You might think that this *machismo* would only be found in older, more traditional Spaniards, but it isn't; some of the younger generation are the same, because they are still brought up to be. And you might think that people in this part of the world would be more used to dealing with foreign women than people elsewhere in the country, but I would say that the macho attitude is the worst in the country here. Perhaps it is a legacy of the several hundred years of North African rule in southern Spain, by very male-dominated dynasties.

The position of women in this part of the world is sometimes still pretty subservient. As an example, I know a Spanish woman who has seven brothers: when she lived at home, she was the only one who ever did any housework. The brothers never lifted a finger to do anything. And even now that she works and lives away from home, she still does washing and cleaning for the two brothers who aren't married. I know another Spanish woman whose husband sits on the settee saying things like, "I'm thirsty – get me a drink." Not only would he not dream of getting it himself, he doesn't even ask politely!

Ivano is half Spanish and half Italian, but he was brought up in Brussels, so he is north European in his attitude to women. It is very different from men brought up here and we see problems in relationships between local men and foreign women. It depends of course on who you are and what you expect, but as a general rule such relationships don't work very well. In Andalusia, men are brought up to be macho and do nothing in the house, while women do everything. I can't see a north European or American woman wanting a relationship like that, unless she likes being dominated.

Doing Business

There are good and bad things about running a business in this country. One of the positives, when compared to Denmark, is the relative freedom you have here. Business practice is very highly controlled and regimented in Denmark and you really have to comply with strict criteria and rules in almost everything you do. There is rather more freedom here to take decisions yourself. I don't mean to bend the rules, or break them (e.g. avoid paying taxes); I just mean freedom to operate your business.

A downside is the red tape and bureaucracy, but something I learned quite early is not to try to deal with this yourself. Even trying to do straightforward things is difficult and you will be told you need to do different things, at different times, by various people. I really believe that it is impossible as an outsider ever to get to grips with the bureaucracy here. So employ a good *gestor* and let him sort all those things out for you. And I recommend that you employ local people to sort out your business for you. They are more in tune with the way things work and the people involved, and hence more likely to achieve things and quickly.

 it is difficult for foreigners to be accepted a hundred per cent, even if they marry a local

You also need to keep on top of all your paperwork – permits, taxes, etc. – if you want to continue in business long-term. Don't be tempted to let it slip. These are general comments, but a specific problem that I have in this business – although it applies to others too – is the insecurity of leaving your merchandise with people, as we do with wine. If customers can't pay or decide not to pay, it can be very difficult to get your money back. You can put an embargo on their premises – a restaurant, say – which means that, when they want to sell, they cannot until they pay you to clear the outstanding debt, but if the person who owes you cannot be found and served with the papers, there is nothing you can do about it, which is a flaw in the system. So business here can be quite uncertain in that sense, and your recourse is effectively limited.

Another difficulty is when it comes to employing people, because social security payments are high and workers have strong rights to compensation when dismissed, after they have been with you for a certain time.

Changing Traditions

Spanish people have probably got mixed feelings about all the foreigners living here. On the one hand, they are grateful for the money and the jobs that we have brought to the region, which was very poor before the foreign invasion, and they respect us economically. On the other hand, it is difficult for them to tell what we are really like and make friends because so few foreigners integrate properly. And I think some Spanish people – certainly the

more traditional ones – probably think that we are a bit too modern in some
of our attitudes and behaviour.

if you work, you will
probably have to work
longer and harder than
in your home country

I have made a lot of my Spanish friends through Ivano. His aunt lives here and
he has been coming to the area since he was a boy, so he has known people for
many years and in that sense is partly a local, which helps. But I think it is
difficult for foreigners to be accepted a hundred per cent, even if they marry a
local. We are still seen as outsiders to some extent and that affects friendship and
integration. The cultures really are pretty different.

The thing that I miss most about Denmark is friends. Friendships here
sometimes seem to be more superficial and harder to maintain than there, but
that might be an age thing. When I was in Denmark, I was younger and single,
with less job responsibility and no daughter. So there was more time for friends.
But even taking that into account, I think friendships are sometimes not as close
here. For example, it is rare to entertain at home; people often go to a restaurant
when they socialise. It is less intimate than when you have somebody to your
house and cook for them; there is more distance.

I also miss the fact that things are so organised in Denmark and you can get
things done more easily and quickly. I always seem to have a long list of
outstanding matters to deal with here, because everything takes so long to
resolve. It isn't like that in Denmark. It's easier to sort out matters and move on
to the next thing. In fact, I think that is why working hours are shorter in
Denmark: you can deal with things more quickly, whereas here you are
constantly having to chase for things. I also miss cultural activities, like the
theatre, which we lack on the Costa del Sol.

But there are certainly plenty of great aspects to living here. For a start, it is very
beautiful, with mountains, beaches, lakes and lots of variety. Where I lived in
Denmark, by contrast, was flat and dull. And the weather is much better, of
course, so you can spend a lot of time outdoors. It gives you more chance to play
sports too, which I enjoy.

One of the bad things about life here is a recent development. Many people
think that this is a good place to bring up children, and in some ways it is. It is
warm, relaxed, child-friendly and generally safe. But I have noticed recently that
the nightlife for local teenagers has become even wilder. It has always gone on

late into the night, but recently kids have become more involved with alcohol and drugs. What particularly concerns me as a mother is the tales I am now hearing about the promiscuity of local girls. It used to be the case when I was young that boys made the running, but that seems to have changed. So I am not sure I am looking forward to my daughter's teenage years.

If you want to come to live here, I would recommend that you visit a few times first, perhaps several, to get to know the place and what living here is like. You also need to make sure that you have something to do – hobbies and interests if you are retired or a definite job or business if you are younger. So many people drift from job to job, or spend their lives in bars, drinking too much. Don't idealise the life here. It isn't perfect and, if you work, you will probably have to work longer and harder than in your home country. Be careful about who you deal with – it's easy to be ripped off. And if you are serious about staying long term, sort out your papers and permits – you will eventually get tripped up if you don't.

A Volcanic Career

Brian Williamson from Nottingham, England, left a
stable lecturer's job to live in a converted car selling
perfumed rock in Spain. Eight years later, he settled
in Alhaurin de la Torre – after discovering that
his UK home had been repossessed.

Since the age of thirty, I had always wanted to live in Spain. As a lecturer and a single parent, I used to come here for a two-month break every summer with my son. We camped on a deserted beach near Cadiz, Robinson Crusoe-style. So in 1992, we moved to Seville to run our business making smelly rock! I had had a well-paid, stable lecturing job in the UK and I gave up that employment and a pension to work with my son producing fragmented volcanic rock.

We used to colour the white stone with a water-based dye, then dry it completely before impregnating it with fragrance. It was costing us a small fortune in electricity to dry the rock in the UK, so we moved to Spain to take advantage of the abundant sunshine, which could be used as our drying tool.

Dry & Wet

When we arrived in Seville, we rented a *finca* (a rural property) with lots of *campo* (land) and were able to dye over a hundred kilos of stones at a time and then spread them out on large plastic sheets to dry.

Unfortunately, we were let down by just about everybody involved in the business: wholesalers, suppliers and banks. And a manufacturer in Barcelona stole our idea and, within around three months, it seemed as if every '100 peseta' shop (the local equivalent of a pound store) was selling fragranced stones. We were hung out to dry, as it were, and left with three and a half tons of rock fragments.

It was time to sit back and reflect for a while. Our stones kept their fragrance for three months, while our competition's fragrance lasted for a day at best. So we had the advantage of quality, but the distinct disadvantage of being virtually penniless. It was then that we met 'Santo'.

You could say that he sniffed us out. We always kept the car loaded with bags of fragranced stones, in readiness to make sales. So the car was permanently perfumed and left a waft of scent wherever we drove. One day, while driving to a bar in Seville, a guy on a moped picked up the smell and out of interest followed us to the bar, where he introduced himself as 'Santo', which is Spanish for 'Saint'.

He called himself this because it seemed to him that he was always ready to help the needy. It might be more accurate to say that he liked to help those down on their luck in the hope that the help would be returned a hundred-fold in the future! He also belived that a child in the village was capable of faith healing and that he had given the child this gift.

Santo (we never found out his real name) became interested in what we were doing, pursued potential sales and even distilled eucalyptus branches to extract the natural oils. He invited us to move our three-metre caravan onto his land, where he farmed a large crayfish lake. There was never any mention of rent, although every so often I had to help him with catching and cleaning the crayfish. But after a while, we noticed that some of our stock was going missing and, after a year or so, we found a stash of our products in the cellar under his house. Without our knowledge, he had registered us as his employees in order to claim some sort of government social payment or grant. He was later rumbled over this but not prosecuted.

From November until May we sold the fragranced stones to shops in Seville and at the weekly Sunday Rastro in the city. Most Spanish cities have these markets, selling second-hand goods. In Seville, the market is held in the red light area and the sales pitches are controlled by local gypsies and much sought after. As outsiders, we had to arrive on Saturday night to set up and then guard the stall throughout the night. Winter nights in Seville can be very cold and we used to make a small bonfire to keep warm and cook chicken and sardines. The fire became something of a gathering place for local drunks, prostitutes and the homeless but, although our car was British plated and therefore a target, it was never damaged or robbed in all the months we attended the Rastro; I think we were considered to be part of 'the team' and hence protected.

the huge bonfire and fiesta
lasted for two days, attracting more
gold bracelets and chains than you
would normally see in a lifetime

From May until November, we travelled all over Spain selling our stones at the annual *ferias* (fairs or festivals). By this time, my son had found a permanent girlfriend and the three-metre caravan became their home for seven months, as well as home to the massive stock of stones, bottles, bags, labels, etc. Where did I live? In the Astra estate car we used to tow the caravan, in which I rebuilt the front passenger seat and rear bench seat in such a way that it dropped down into a single bed. I later made an built-in bar and wardrobe unit!

We travelled around Spain, from Burgos in the north to Cadiz in the south, setting up in a different *feria* each week, selling the stones. I kept a diary, because one day I wanted to adapt the stories into a book, which I also thought would make a good TV sitcom. On one occasion, the caravan left the tow bar and sank into an irrigation ditch. The roof was just visible above the water and, to add insult to injury, the Guardia Civil accused me of operating a boat in restricted water. They thought that the roof was the wheelhouse of a boat!

On another occasion, we spent a Christmas on a site next to some Romany gypsies and were invited to their celebrations, which was a huge honour and quite an experience. Theirs is a completely different culture; the huge bonfire and fiesta lasted for two days, attracting more gold bracelets and chains than you would normally see in a lifetime.

Conmen, Drug-Traffickers & Spies

During this early time in Spain, my house in the UK was being rented out. But after a year or so, a conman talked the people renting the house into paying him the rental money. As a result, the mortgage wasn't paid and by the time I became aware of the problem, the building society was repossessing the property. I lost £50,000 and the house was sold to a sister company of the building society for its mortgage value. While this was undoubtedly morally wrong, a solicitor advised me that it would take two years to fight the case, and I couldn't afford that time away from Spain. When I came back here, the gypsies offered to visit the building society in the UK and sort the problem out in their way!

*'is this your suitcase, sir?' asked
the airport administrator sharply,
his chubby cheeks wobbling in
a vaguely menacing way*

We spent nearly eight years travelling around Spain and had some fascinating experiences. One that sticks in my mind is being offered a fee to drive more than £100,000-worth of drugs to Madrid. I refused. But after the eight years of travelling, we decided to buy a property and are now settled, with a villa in Alhaurin de la Torre (a town inland from Malaga) and another which we rent out. My son owns an artists' shop in the coastal town of Fuengirola, full of hand-made products which cannot be found elsewhere. As for me, well, I work harder than ever – helping in my son's shop and managing the letting of our second villa – but I don't get paid so often now!

The second villa, incidentally, we purchased from an ex-spy, who worked for the UK, when he was younger (he is over 80 now). He is a fascinating man, full of stories, but naturally keeps a low profile. The villa is on the top of a hill, with 360-degree views, and we rent it out during the summer. So our life has undergone quite a transition, from a traditional life in the UK with a stable salary, to a life of survival in Spain and, recently, relative stability here.

A Toxic Tale

The following is a cautionary tale for the many who fly regularly between the UK and Spain and who fail to pay enough attention to the contents of their luggage. It is also a warning to anyone who enjoys my hobby of making ceramic models!

One cold, overcast January morning, as I approached the departure lounge at Heathrow's Terminal Two, I couldn't have known the chaos that I was about to unleash on myself and others. I had arrived just over an hour and a half before my departure time, and my flight to Malaga was being checked in. The queue at the check-in desk wasn't too long and my single case was soon tagged and unceremoniously trundled away into the bowels of the airport. I then went to the departure lounge and bought a magazine to read while waiting to board my flight. My relaxed state was short-lived.

"Will a Mr Brian Williamson travelling on flight DKL 324 to Malaga please go urgently to baggage control," came the announcement.

When I managed eventually to locate baggage control (a large office which appeared to have been recently ravaged by Hurricane Billy) I spotted my burgundy case on a metal table near the door. A security guard, a rather bulky police officer and an administrator with large cheeks stood soberly guarding the offending case. I scanned their faces quickly; it was obvious that I wasn't being nominated for a prize.

"Is this your suitcase, sir?" asked the airport administrator sharply, his chubby cheeks wobbling in a vaguely menacing way.

There was little or no doubt about the answer. No other suitcase had hand-painted yellow triangles on each corner. "Yes," I replied with absolute conviction.

The case had already been unzipped. The security officer pulled it open and with a grace, poise and art that would have pleased Sherlock Holmes, withdrew a one-litre aluminium canister.

"Is this your property, sir?" the guard enquired solemnly.

"Yes," I replied, this time with more than a hint of guilt.

"Why are you carrying this canister?" snapped the guard, obviously feeling a need to prolong the interrogation.

Now came my moment and I had to make it sound good, with all eyes focused on me. "It contains a type of liquid plastic, which when mixed with a catalyst solidifies, and I want to experiment with making transparent models with the resin," was my cautious reply.

"Did you know, sir, that this material needs a special permit to be transported by a civilian airliner?" the administrator asked bluntly. "It's classified as a toxic substance."

To tell the truth, I had never given this possibility a thought, despite the label on the back bearing a large red and black cross. It was time to grovel, admit guilt and explain that no malicious intent had been involved.

"Fine, sir. We accept you explanation, but you must act more responsibly in future!" was the reply. "Your case will be put on the aircraft, but the canister will not. I suggest that you hurry because passengers will shortly be boarding."

As I began to leave the office, a sharp voice called me back. "Excuse me, sir. This is your canister. We don't want it left here."

There were sixty-five minutes left before the departure of my flight. I hurried across the departure area, searching for the airport police office. I would explain the situation and leave the troublesome canister with them.

Walking around one of the world's largest airports carrying a distinctly bomb-like canister is almost bound to attract attention, and armed airport security police were soon escorting me to their inner sanctum!

The senior officer was pleasant enough but unsympathetic to my predicament. "Try left luggage, sir," was his suggestion. "And please put the canister in this plastic bag to avoid any further upsets."

So I was back in circulation, with fifty-two precious minutes remaining. I became more and more irritated as I filled in the long-term left luggage form. A sulky, dark-haired woman examined the form and announced that the canister couldn't be left with her because it contained a toxic substance. I argued a little and, checking my watch, saw that only forty minutes remained until my flight departed. "Besides," she added, "how do I know that the canister isn't a bomb?"

"Because the canister is well known to all the security staff at this airport and isn't a bomb!" I replied, by now nervous and more than a touch irritated.

"Then leave it with them," she snapped at me.

I left. I wondered whether I could simply pour the liquid plastic down the toilet. I quickly realised that this was a silly idea as it would pollute the watercourse. As for just leaving the canister in the toilet, I was sure that its presence would quickly be reported, and my mind was filled with visions of airport closures and controlled explosions.

By now, there were a mere thirty-five minutes left and I almost ran across the departure area. The information board was flashing 'last boarding' for flight DKL 324. Panic began to take hold and I was sweating. I was running out of options. Curse the canister, curse model making and curse airports!

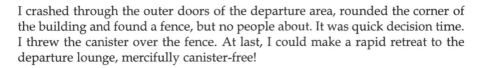

> *due to the circumstances of our life here, I have met people that I would never have talked to had I remained a lecturer*

I crashed through the outer doors of the departure area, rounded the corner of the building and found a fence, but no people about. It was quick decision time. I threw the canister over the fence. At last, I could make a rapid retreat to the departure lounge, mercifully canister-free!

Alas not!

The security cameras scanning the building's perimeter meant that armed guards were despatched to my position before I could re-enter the departure lounge. What a moment to make my television debut! My embarrassment was even greater than the panic I felt about missing my flight. One of the guards, who had questioned me earlier, simply told me to pick up the canister and leave. Instead, I asked him to accompany me to a nearby taxi rank. This he did and then explained the situation to a bewildered cabbie. The last I saw of the canister, it was sitting on the front seat of the cab beside two twenty pound notes headed for the local refuse dump.

But did I catch the flight? The aircraft was delayed because it couldn't leave with my case on board, but not me. Crew and passengers are normally upset by such delays, but my situation was an exception and I was treated with some respect. After all, how many passengers are escorted onto an aircraft by three armed security guards? My fellow passengers were too intrigued to be upset.

Ups & Downs

Because I had first known Spain from a tourist's point of view, coming out here for two-month holidays and then returning to work in the UK, it was a big shock to be here and faced with the need to earn a living. As you can tell from our experiences, we have had a few ups and downs.

One of the biggest downs occurred when I invested over £6,000 in Ocaso Insurance Spain. The receptionist gave me a counter-signed receipt, but the money actually ended up in his pocket. It turned out that the receipt was invalid, so I lost all the money! The company told me that my problem was with the individual concerned, not with them. When I investigated taking legal action, I found that it would be expensive, so I gave up pursuing the matter.

I am not too fond of some of the daft rules and regulations that we have in Spain, and the general uncertainty that seems to surround when and whether they apply or not. I am also not a great fan of Spanish beer and I now find the summers too hot here, so I might consider returning to the UK for future ones, although I seem to get bored there so quickly.

Life is better in Spain. For a start, we live surrounded by countryside and animals. And with two plots of around 4,000 square metres each, gardening has become a hobby. I don't have a choice really! But learning has been a wonderful experience with all the new plants.

The pace of life in Spain is so much more relaxed and the settled weather means that a weekly barbecue with friends is a must in the summer, with plenty of *tinto de verano* (red wine mixed with lemonade or soda), of course. I like living inland, around fifteen minutes from the sea, but nowhere near the beach bars and tourist hordes. We're in real Spain.

As for neighbours, my advice is to not get too close because, if you fall out with them, it can be a disaster. Stay good but distant friends with them if possible. Of course, I often talk to my neighbours, but we aren't always popping round for coffee. As for friends, making them is easy in Spain, and many of mine are oddballs! Due to the circumstances of our life here, I have met people that I would never have talked to had I remained a lecturer. For example, I know fire eaters, clowns, circus trainers, religious leaders, radio presenters, TV people and many others – a wide variety.

> **try to make sure that family members don't use your house automatically every year for a free holiday**

I also have Spanish friends and, on the whole, foreigners in Alhaurin de la Torre tend to speak some Spanish and try to integrate, which Spanish people do appreciate. I suppose that a downside of our presence here is that we have caused house prices to rise; also, all too often, foreigners are intolerant of Spanish customs.

To anybody thinking of coming to live in Spain, my advice is to rent for a year first and to talk to as many people as possible, but believe none of them totally. Learn as much as you can and then find a good solicitor or *gestor* with a proven track record. Be flexible and prepared to give and take. Try to learn at least some Spanish and avoid the know-it-alls in the coastal bars – and the inland bars come to that. Be independent and choose your friends very carefully. Try to make sure that family members don't use your house automatically every year for a free holiday – make only limited offers. And, last but not least, make sure that you keep a decent link with the UK for all those 'essentials', like pork pies!

Happy Penury

Margaret Crawford and her 13-year-old daughter
moved from North Wales to Marbella to attend
the same school. Her meagre salary means no
holidays, no going out and no television.

The decision to come to Spain was very much that of my two daughters, not mine. I had concluded that we needed a change of scene following my divorce from the girls' father (even though he and I have remained friends) but I had imagined that we would stay in Britain. In fact, I didn't think we would go much further from our North Wales home than Bangor or Chester, so a move to Spain has been much more radical than I had envisaged. The idea was sown by Maisie, who had always loved coming to Spain on holiday. We used to come most years because my ex-husband's mother lives here and, every time we returned to Wales, Maisie used to pine for Spain.

My daughters realised that I would need pushing in order to do something about moving, so they took a 'proactive' approach. The older one, Alice, began to scan the overseas job advertisements in the *Times Educational Supplement*. I pooh-poohed this because of my intention to move somewhere no more distant or exotic than Chester! The 'trouble' began when Alice spotted an advertisement for a teaching post at an elementary school in the Marbella area. I thought the girls were mad even to consider such a thing, but they began jumping up and down with excitement, so to calm them down I rang the number in the advert. To my amazement, and slight horror, somebody answered. I spoke to them about the job and they asked me to send my CV.

Soon after I had put down the phone, a neighbour came round and said that I could use their fax machine to send the CV, which was duly despatched, within a mere hour of Alice spotting the advertisement. Shortly afterwards, the school phoned back to ask me to attend an interview. I explained that we would be coming to Spain anyway in a couple of weeks for a holiday and that I would come and see them then. At that stage, I was still thinking that none of this was actually serious and that I would go along to the interview simply to shut the girls up, but it somehow seemed to take on a robust momentum of its own.

Facing The Inevitable

A couple of weeks later, I, the two girls and two other family members turned up at the school in Marbella. While I was being interviewed, the others were given a guided tour of the school, which they loved. The headmistress later said that she had liked the look of me the moment I got out of the car, so it all appeared to be heading towards an inevitable conclusion. And then they offered me the job and it all seemed too outrageously silly to be true. Not only could I not envisage moving to Spain, but Alice would have to stay behind in England to finish her A Level studies. But my attitude towards the idea gradually began to soften, probably partly as a result of persistent barracking by the girls.

My family was very open to the idea of my emigrating, but most of them have travelled, some extensively, and they probably wondered why I hadn't broken out of the home environment earlier. On the other hand, they wondered about the Costa del Sol as a destination, because they thought of it as a bit tatty, which parts of it certainly are. One of my sisters, at least, has changed her mind since, because she and her husband have recently bought a house here.

> *some people seemed almost resentful that we were thinking of going abroad and that it must reflect badly on them*

The attitude of some friends was also negative. Certain of them had the narrow, judgemental attitude sometimes found in rural communities the world over. Some of the older people in the community had never travelled more than about twenty-five miles from where they were born, so somebody contemplating a move abroad must have appeared to be from another planet. Some people seemed almost resentful that we were thinking of going abroad and that it must reflect badly on them, that they couldn't be good enough for us. Others just thought it was a reaction to the divorce and that we would be back within a month or so, with our tails between our legs.

By now, I had decided that we should go for a year and see how it went, and accordingly signed a year's contract with the school. We kept our house in Wales, so we knew that we would have something to go back to if it went pear-shaped.

Three years later, we are still at the same school and loving it.

Disappearing Pupils

It isn't a Spanish state school but a private one, and it attracts mostly children with middle-class, professional parents from near and far: Malaga, Holland, Britain, Russia, Sweden, Finland and India, to name but a few places. All teaching at the school is done in English, and children are allowed to speak only English, except in Spanish classes.

Having worked in the education systems in both Britain and Spain, I would say that standards are higher here. The school concentrates on core subjects – English, maths and science – and teaching isn't bogged down with all the fripperies that you find in Britain, like assemblies, politics, bureaucracy and national curriculum this, that and the other.

Children in Spain are at a higher level than they are in the UK and, when Maisie arrived at the age of eleven, she found it tough to catch up; and she is an academically gifted girl. (I'm not just saying that because I'm her parent, but as a teacher – honestly!) I would say that the six-year-olds (I teach children between six and eight) are up to two years ahead of their compatriots in Britain. For example, they are already doing joined-up script at that age.

Even though Spanish schools stick to core subjects, their approach to education is flexible and relaxed. In fact, I would describe it as a proper form of education, rather than just preparing children to take exams, based rigidly around a national curriculum, as is all too often the case in Britain. For example, a couple of weeks ago, a lizard appeared in the classroom, so I went to find a science teacher, and he came and told the children all about lizards, with the planned lesson postponed. We have that flexibility here and the chance to improvise, which is greatly to the benefit of the pupils' education. I think that I have been allowed to learn how to teach properly out here.

> **you wonder what their parents have done, or not done, to lead to such a precipitous flight from Spain**

Two downsides of the school where I work are the transience of the staff and pupils, and the fact that children can study only a limited number of subjects at O Level. Some foreign teachers are here only for a short while, as they are working their way around the world, teaching here and there as they go. (Others are only really in Spain for the lifestyle, and that is perhaps their focus rather than the teaching itself.) And some of our pupils come and go with surprising speed; almost alarming speed, in fact. I realise that much of the foreign adult population on the Costa del Sol is transient, but some of the children are pulled out of school with no notice at all and not heard from again. You wonder what their parents have done, or not done, to lead to such a precipitous flight from Spain! But in such circumstances, it is best not to ask any questions, although you do worry about the well-being of the children concerned.

As for the limited number of O Levels available to take at the school, that is because we have a limited number of teachers, some of them offering more than one subject. I think we might return to Britain some time before the run up to Maisie's O Levels, to give her a greater choice of subjects, especially some of the creative ones. As to whether we go back permanently or full-time, who knows?

Local Colour

There has never been a time when either of us has regretted coming to Spain, so we must have settled in quite well. The first property we rented here backed onto a sheltered valley, which was full of birds and wildlife. We loved gazing at the views and also found that when you get out of bed in the morning in such an environment you feel great, more alive in fact. I think it is partly because of the light and open skies in southern Spain. When we went back to Britain last Christmas, we quickly felt oppressed by the lack of sunshine and the low, grey skies. In fact, we took the lampshades off the lights where we were staying and replaced the light bulbs with brighter ones in order to get more light into our lives! And we missed the colourful plants which grow here all year. Poor old England seemed monotone by comparison.

Learning the language was always going to be an important part of trying to settle in Spain, and Maisie has done very well. I think it only took her about six months to learn to speak it pretty well. She doesn't really remember learning; it just sort of happened. When we first came, she spoke no Spanish whatever and used to communicate with Spanish children with sign language, and it just sort of grew from there.

I think it helped that she had learned Welsh and English as a child and was therefore used to different languages. She was so good at Welsh that she was going to take her exams in it if we had stayed. Here in Spain, if there is a group of children of different nationalities – say three or four English children and a Spaniard – they all speak Spanish.

I go to Spanish classes once a week but I haven't yet got the confidence to use my Spanish much. Another thing I have had trouble getting used to here is the driving. Where we lived in Wales, there was only one main street and I had never seen heavy traffic before, let alone driven over here, on the 'wrong' side of the road and with so many other cars. So I was very nervous the first time I took to the roads in Spain, and it was only an exploratory trip to the local shops! But I have gradually got used to it since, which is a good job because I drive to and from work every day.

Rude Childcare

One of the things that has helped us to settle here is the fact that people seem to like children in Spain. Adults respect children in this country, whereas in Britain kids are often effectively told to 'piss off'. People talk to children here, take notice of them and don't see them as being in the way. I see this attitude at school every day. You would expect teachers to have a rapport with children, but the ancillary staff are the same. They absolutely love the children.

Children definitely come first in this country. You notice it in little details. There are kiosks here that sell sweets, which have little platforms for smaller children to stand on so that they can see over the counter. It's a thoughtful touch and typical of Spain. But even though children are very well looked after here, they are also given a lot of freedom. There aren't too many restrictions and aren't over-protected.

In Britain, by contrast, there are warning signs and ropes cordoning things off, cosseting people all the time. Maisie made a good point recently, that she thinks children brought up in Spain would cope better with a crisis than those brought up in Britain, because they are allowed to think for themselves here and learn to cope with things.

It is a late-night culture for children in this country. When we arrived and Maisie was eleven, she used to stay up and play outside until late, which is normal in the Spanish community. Now her curfew time is midnight, and when she is fifteen she will go into town at night.

I think that children here tend to be better behaved than British children. British kids often seem to lack respect for anybody or anything and they don't know how to behave in public. Spanish teenagers don't tend to dress and act like urban guerrillas, unlike their British counterparts.

The health service in Spain appears to be impressive and they don't mess around, but get right down to treating you, robustly. Our first exposure to this was when Maisie had an infected mosquito bite, probably because she had been picking at it. The bite grew alarmingly, until it was about two centimetres across and obviously badly infected. We took her to the emergency room, where they took one look at it, decided that action was required and promptly ripped the scab off with some tweezers. There was no preamble or gentle build-up, just decisive action, which verged on the abrupt.

The doctor then called an assistant to hold Maisie's arm, to stop her flinching or pulling away, and she scrubbed the wound as if she was going at an old pair of shoes with a brush. Poor Maisie's eyes were practically rolling in her head, but the two medics were unmoved, talking over her – about traffic I think. They then produced some clear liquid, which we assumed would be a pleasant, soothing balm after the rough and tumble of the tweezer-ripping and the nail brush treatment, but when they put it in the cleaned wound, it frothed and fizzed, reacting as it came into contact with the bacteria, which had obviously penetrated quite deeply into Maisie's arm. It's like tough love, I suppose: fast, thorough and punchy, which is a good way to approach things. I approve.

Getting By

Spanish people in general are very sympathetic. They have a good understanding of humanity and accept the differences in people. They are caring, they look out for each other and they try to sort problems out by discussion rather than confrontation. The Spanish aren't generally aggressive and I think they sometimes find that the British, en masse, can be. In fact, one of the few things we don't like about life on the Costa del Sol is the behaviour of uncouth Brits. By no means all Britons here are like that, of course, but some certainly are.

The other quibble is salaries, which are low: I earn a mere third of my old UK salary, so I have to supplement it by taking pupils in the evenings and at weekends. I work long hours, still for not much reward: we are up at 7am and the day usually doesn't finish until 8pm. Life is probably cheaper here than it is in Britain, but not that much cheaper – not enough to compensate for the lower wages. We get by, but not by much, and there is no emergency fund.

> *my daughter and I are closer now; we discuss everything, we row a lot, but we work things out in the end*

When we have more spare cash, we would like to travel more within Spain, which is a wonderful country. I love Seville; it's a beautiful city, resembling an outdoor museum. But I think we will avoid going again in the summer. I have just read that in June this year, the temperature reached 50°C (122°F), which is nothing less than alarming. But you don't have to travel too far from the Costa del Sol to find very beautiful scenery and a completely different feel to the coast. Not far north of Malaga is a beautiful limestone region called El Torcal, with amazing rock formations sculpted by the weather, and the nearby El Chorro gorge is dramatic too.

Because of the shortage of funds, we rarely go out and I haven't had a boyfriend here. It doesn't bother me and it has had an interesting effect on my relationship with Maisie. We are closer now; we discuss everything, we row a lot, but we work things out in the end. We communicate all the time and, not having TV, we don't fall back on that; and children in Spain generally don't seem to have as much of a TV culture as they do in Britain. So these aspects of Spanish life are having a beneficial effect on us and long may it continue.

Cut Off On The Costa Blanca

Mark Jacobs was brought up in South Africa,
by British and American parents. He came to the
Altea region of the Costa Blanca in search of
an alternative home, but the one he chose
brought him a sense of isolation.

I travelled extensively when I worked in the travel business and always intended to live away from South Africa, at least for a while. Many South Africans do, often in Britain if they are of British origin. But Spain has always appealed to me, partly because of the weather. It is difficult to grow up in a climate like South Africa's and then move to a place like Britain, with grey, chilly skies and drizzle. And Spain's Mediterranean coast has weather similar to Cape Town's, where I lived for many years.

Coming here was partly a desire to live in another country and culture, but also as a possible escape from South Africa if it 'caught fire', in a similar way to Zimbabwe, with land grabs and the persecution of whites. I am very pleased to say that South Africa seems to have stabilised and to be doing well, but I didn't want to take a chance and wanted to plan an alternative at a time of my choosing and on my own terms, not somebody else's. There is also a question of geography. After our divorce, my ex-wife and daughters moved to the UK – they live in Yorkshire – so I am much closer to them in Spain than if I had remained in Cape Town, which is a twelve-hour flight from Heathrow.

Escape To Isolation

I chose the Costa Blanca rather than elsewhere else in Spain because I wanted to live near the sea and liked the fact that sections of this coast are still quite undeveloped. I also read that some organisation like the World Health Authority had said it had one of the healthiest climates in the world, and South Africans like to spend a lot of time in the great outdoors in warm sunshine. I was also pleased to discover how warm and shark-free the water is. The sea off Cape Town is always pretty chilly – most surfers wear wetsuits – and the sharks have been active recently. Some poor child lost a leg a couple of months ago and attacks are increasing, possibly because of the increasing popularity of 'shark cage' diving trips: they chum the water (bait it with fish blood and bits) to attract sharks, so the sharks associate man with food, which is bad news if you are a human in the water with them.

Having travelled so much, I thought it would be easy to settle in Spain, so I was surprised when it was harder than expected. Looking back, I think I tried to do too many things at once. I went through a divorce, sold two of my properties in South Africa (I still keep an apartment in Cape Town) and then emigrated to a different continent, all one after the other. And, shortly after that, I decided to retire. It was a lot to handle in a short time. I think I might have felt the restlessness and sense of isolation, which I felt here at first, to some extent if I had stayed in South Africa, but not as acutely.

I suddenly went from being very busy, selling properties and tying up various interests in South Africa, to being on my own in a large villa in Spain. In South

Africa, I had lived in the centre of Cape Town, surrounded by friends. Here, I knew nobody, except my estate agent and lawyer, and was living out in the semi-countryside. The first couple of weeks, I hardly spoke to anybody. I called on the two neighbouring villas to introduce myself but both owners were away – it was summer and they had headed north to avoid the heat. Even the estate agent and lawyer were on holiday.

> *even though I am from a country with eleven official languages, I am not one of life's natural linguists*

Nothing much happens or gets done on the Costa Blanca until the summer tourist season ends in mid-September, so I pulled myself together and set myself some short-term goals: to lose the extra weight I had piled on over the previous year, to sort out the garden (which would be the main way of losing weight) and to study Spanish intensively. I had done some studying while in South Africa, but not as much as I had intended and my knowledge was basic.

In At The Deep End

So I spent my first month doing that and then the children came out for a visit, along with friends from England, which helped a lot. After that, when 'normal' life resumed after the summer madness, I threw myself into life in Spain. I took a Spanish class, became a regular at local bars and restaurants and joined several informal clubs, for hiking, bridge, watercolour painting and wining and dining. I had read that when somebody is bereaved or divorced and wants to get back on their feet, they should accept every invitation they are given. So I took that advice and accepted pretty much everything, no matter how much I didn't like the sound of it.

You get to meet a lot of people that way. Some of them you don't like, of course, but plenty you do. And now I have a wide circle of friends – Britons, Danes, Germans, Finns and Spaniards – although my creaky Spanish holds me back with the natives. Even though I am from a country with eleven official languages, I have discovered that I am not one of life's natural linguists. I don't seem able to tune my ear to it, which you have to do. You mustn't try to pick out every word when somebody is talking, because they have said another dozen words while you are still wrestling with an earlier one. So you have to pick up key words and try to get the general meaning of what is being said rather than the exact meaning of the whole thing – easier said than done. I am too conscious about making errors; you mustn't be and just have to plough on.

Age is against me too – it is apparently much easier to learn a language when you are younger.

One thing that really gets to some foreigners in this country and makes settling in difficult is the *mañana* attitude, but that isn't going to shock South Africans, who are well used to what is called 'African time', whereby things always take longer than they are meant to and proceed by a more tortuous route than hoped for. Capetonians sometimes take this further and refer to 'Cape Town African time', which adds an extra touch of the city's laid-back nature, meaning that things take even longer. So I have been well trained for *mañana*. That is not to say that I like it, but it hasn't come as a shock.

I have found most people in this area to be very friendly, Spanish and foreign alike. That is something else that attracted me here because Cape Town has a laid-back, sociable feel to the place and people are relaxed and friendly, and you get that here too. The beautiful surroundings and weather seem to put people in a good frame of mind and they have time to talk. And I suppose the foreigners who come to live here must be more open-minded than average or they wouldn't have left home.

a lot of expats have little or no involvement with the Spanish community and lead quite narrow lives

I have come across the odd person who has a problem with white South Africans, but that isn't unusual. Ten years into South African democracy, I think a lot of people accept that most of us were glad to see the back of apartheid, although some aggressively 'politically correct' sorts will always be suspicious. I was recently quoted a song lyric from the old British TV satirical comedy series 'Spitting Image': "I've never met a nice South African". It was done in jest but I think some folk are still influenced by that and are surprised that most of us are quite nice! I find that people who have visited South Africa, particularly Cape Town, have been impressed by the openness and friendliness of the people.

What I would say about friendships here – and it applies to expatriate communities anywhere – is that people sometimes become friends with others more because they are from the same country or share the same golf club than because they are natural soul mates. A lot of expats have little or no involvement with the Spanish community and lead quite narrow lives, involving visiting each other's homes for drinks, playing golf or tennis, and patronising a limited number of English-speaking bars and restaurants.

There are some people who criticise those foreigners in Spain who stick to their own community, whether British, Scandinavian, German or whatever. But I don't think it is right to do that. If people want to live life like that, fine. We might think they are missing out by not trying to get involved with Spain and Spanishness, but who is to say that they should? Immigrant groups all over the world tend to stick to their own, so it is nothing new. And the foreigners here have brought a lot of jobs and money to Spain.

Efficiency & Expropriation

South Africans are used to having their own medical insurance because the public health service in South Africa is very limited and overused, and I have got private cover here. So my experience with the Spanish public system is nil. But that might change, because I have recently been told that the public sector pays better than the private one and so attracts better doctors. This seems unlikely, but I am going to investigate it further!

From what I gather from friends, both foreign and Spanish, the care given in the public health system is of a high or very high standard. I think the doctors can seem brusque to foreigners who are used to a bit more 'tender loving care', but almost everybody is impressed by their efficiency and the treatment they receive. The one quibble patients have is the length of time you have to wait to see your doctor. But waiting is part of life in this country. I have also heard that pressures are increasing on the health system because of the number of foreign retirees coming to live in Spain part or fulltime, and older people usually take up more medical time and resources than younger ones, except the very young.

I like to think that not too much in life surprises me any more, but Spanish property regulations and laws certainly do, particularly in this part of Spain. I have read about property irregularities and strange laws in other parts of Spain – for example involving the late Jesus Gil, former mayor of Marbella – and also about the number of buildings without planning permission in parts of Andalusia, but the Valencia region has really surpassed itself on this issue.

That is because of something which has emotively been called the 'Valencia land grab law'. Its official name is the *Ley Reguladora de la Actividad Urbanistica* and it was a law passed by the Valencia state government in 1994 to help speed up urban development. Under local laws, land is classified as land already urbanised, land suitable for urbanisation or rural land. It is quite common in many countries for rural land to be reclassified as suitable for being built on when the demand for property is high.

The law was brought in to prevent owners of rural property standing in the way of developments that were deemed to be of benefit to the general community, for example additional housing and improvements to services and amenities. Further, the law deemed that, because the value of their properties would increase as a result of the improved local infrastructure, the owners of the rural properties were obliged to contribute, either financially or by ceding land, towards the cost of the benefits, e.g. new roads, sewage systems, etc., regardless of whether they wanted the new facilities or not.

The idea was to make sure that developments were constructed with adequate attendant services and facilities, including roads, sanitation, green belts and other things. But the legislation was badly put together and it has been used by sharp property developers to expropriate land or give people massive bills for 'urbanising' their land.

The law means that property developers can ask that land is reclassified from rural to urban without the owner's permission. That also happens in other countries, including Great Britain, but in Valencia developers can buy the land compulsorily from the owners after the reclassification, usually for a stupidly low price. Again as in Great Britain, it is a legal requirement that notices of intent be published, but a mere fifteen days are given to present an alternative plan or an objection and, because many landowners are absentees or foreign, they aren't around to do so. Besides that, the alternative plans submitted by residents are frequently turned down and some people see this as dodgy mutual back-scratching by developers and corrupt local government officials.

The 'harshest' version of the law applies in the provinces of Alicante, Valencia and Castellón, which includes the Costa del Azahar and the Costa Blanca and their hinterlands. Other parts of Spain apparently have less punitive versions, which don't seem to cause problems, but you never know about the future and laws of course can change, particularly when money is involved.

Fortunately, a campaign led by a group called *Abusos Urbanistico No* and some Spanish and British MEPs has made the Valencia government agree to amend the law and strengthen the hand of small landowners. This should take place some time in 2004. But until it happens, it is safest to buy property on land already classified as urban. And always employ a good lawyer to protect your interests and inform you of any potential problems with land or property purchase.

Cons & Common Sense

I also think you should be careful with the estate agent you do business with, because I have heard stories about fly-by-night operators, some dealing via the internet. Some of them set up online in order to avoid paying Spanish taxes and they require commission to be paid in cash. You should be suspicious of any company that doesn't have a VAT number (called a *CIF*) and that doesn't list the names of the principals and have a genuine address. You should deal only with those that have an office where they can be contacted or 'tied down'.

It also helps if the agent is a member of one of the professional organisations, such as API and FOPDAC. And be clear (in writing) from the start exactly what the agent's fees are – including VAT. Watch out for agents who try to draw up contracts of sale with both the buyer and the seller, in order to pull the wool over both sides' eyes as to the real price and inflate their commission. And always employ a lawyer, even if the agent says it isn't necessary; in fact, **especially** if the agent says it is unnecessary!

 foreigners in Spain sometimes appear to have left their common sense at home

I am not claiming to be anything like an expert on buying and selling land and property in Spain, or anywhere for that matter, so double-check with a lawyer that what I have written is still the case. Even if it isn't a hundred per cent accurate or current, it shows the pitfalls that can affect the purchaser of property in this beautiful part of the world. If nothing else, it will hopefully convince people of the need to find and use a reliable lawyer when buying property here. Not doing so could prove to be a very false economy.

I have noticed that foreigners in Spain sometimes appear to have left their common sense at home and do ridiculous things when it comes to buying and selling properties and businesses. You need to have your wits about you in this part of the world: check everything and don't trust others to be of good faith – there are con artists about. The warm weather and relaxed atmosphere in Spain seem to lull people into a false sense of security, to the point where they think that 'nothing can go wrong here'. Sorry, folks, but it can and sometimes does.

Escape From Isolation

I am intending to change the way I live, by selling the villa, which is too big for one person, even though the space is useful when guests come to stay. Instead, I will buy an apartment or townhouse nearer to a town, or in a quiet part of a town, where I will stay for about half the year – the cooler half. It will be more secure and easier to lock up than the villa when I am away.

My decision not to live in Spain for the whole year isn't due to the fact that I don't like it here – I do – but because there are so many other places to live. And the summer tourist season on the Costa Blanca, which is really from Easter to October, can be very hot and crowded, as in resort areas in the rest of Spain. I have found it a bit much to put up with, even if you are half hidden from the crowds and craziness by living in a villa, as I have been. The problems come when you need or want to venture out. So I will be spending the warmer months elsewhere from this year – they are great for the tourists but not so good for the people living here, unless they run a bar or restaurant and want the business. I will spend some of the Spanish summer back in South Africa and the rest in northern Europe, including spending more time with the children in Britain.

> *Spain is one of the world's better countries to live in. However, it isn't the paradise that some expatriates seem to paint it as*

If you are after a tranquil retirement and don't want too much to do, this part of the world is wonderful. But if, like me you are after a bit more, it can be limiting. I think it is partly my age (47): I am just not ready to sit back yet and watch the world go by. And I do wonder if some of the retired people in Spain get bored but don't realise it.

The main thing I got wrong was to buy a property without having rented first. I think I was a bit snooty about it, thinking renting to be a bit low grade, which is stupid, but I am used to owning my own home. My advice is to get over that feeling and definitely rent first. You might think that you want a large villa, as I did, but you might find it unsuitable. Mine is too big for one person and the gardens and pool are a constant source of work, even if you have people to help.

Large properties need regular minor work to keep them in a decent state. The experts say you need to spend at least one or two per cent of the value of the property on repairs and alterations every year, to keep it in good order. And the strong sunshine in this part of the world takes its toll on properties, especially woodwork and painted and varnished surfaces. The most labour-intensive job is probably painting the bars and barred gates that protect windows and doors on a lot of properties in Spain.

So owning a large home is quite a tie, and having one usually means you are located a bit out of things, away from the action. I always have to drive if I want to go anywhere and that is a bit of a bore, especially as I like a drink. And you have to be careful about that in this country. I think some foreigners think it is fine to run around in the car half-cut and that the police don't mind, but they do.

Spain has some of the worst traffic accident rates in Europe, which has embarrassed the authorities and they have been cracking down recently because a lot of the accidents are apparently caused by drunk drivers. And the legal blood/alcohol level is low in Spain, lower than in the UK, for example.

We foreigners should make more of an effort to learn the language properly. It will make you stand out because so few do and Spanish speakers tend to pay less for services, whether car repairs, plumbing, carpentry or whatever, because they can use locals and hence have a lot more choice. You will also be better able to understand and take part in local festivities. Spain has plenty of fiestas and ferias, and you should throw yourself into them, as the locals do.

Having travelled a lot, I would say that Spain is one of the world's better countries to live in. However, it isn't the paradise that some expatriates seem to paint it as – usually the newly arrived ones or those who have sold up everything in their original country and cannot afford to return. So don't expect everything to be perfect. The Valencia property situation described earlier is an example of the problems the country can throw at you. But it is mainly a civilised place to live, especially when the beach tourists have departed for the season.

Unchained Melody

Caroline Larkin moved from north-west England to
Marbella to begin her career as a music teacher.
After giving up her job and getting a divorce, she has
learned that life in Spain isn't always harmonious.

I came to Spain because of music, after doing a degree in it at a British university. When I finished the course, I couldn't decide whether I wanted to teach music or play in an orchestra. If I had wanted to teach, it would have meant an extra year of study to gain a qualification and I also fancied a gap year, so I decided to opt for playing; I knew that I could always train to teach at a later stage. I also wanted to spend a year abroad and initially thought about either Germany or Italy, two countries with strong classical music traditions. It was completely by chance that I ended up in Spain.

An Inauspicious Start

I was queuing for concert tickets in London and got talking to the woman next to me, who turned out to be from Marbella. She mentioned that the classical music scene in southern Spain was developing, with new orchestras planned for Malaga and Seville, the latter as part of Expo 92, which was held there.

Shortly after this meeting, at which we had exchanged telephone numbers, she rang to tell me that they were holding orchestral auditions in Malaga the following week and to send over my CV. That was in November 1990, when I was twenty-one. I had recently moved back in with my parents in the north-west of England, I was working at Victoria Wines at night, my friends all seemed to be getting exciting jobs and the early winter weather was getting me down. So the prospect of a trip to Spain was very appealing, particularly as I had never been before.

So off I went and stayed with the family of the lady I had met in the concert ticket queue. But the trip began inauspiciously. We travelled from Marbella to Malaga (about an hour's drive) for the audition, but I hadn't taken my passport with me, for the simple reason that I hadn't been told it was required. But in Spain you always have to carry identification and need to present it for just about anything you want to do. Everybody was amazed that I hadn't known this. So they refused to let me audition, even though I had come all the way from Britain!

Eventually they relented and allowed me to audition – last. I managed to play well despite the unexpected hassle, but they didn't offer me a contract because they had already filled all the full-time places. They did, however, offer me a fill-in position, in which I would act as a sort of locum. It was unsatisfactory really, but I accepted, and have played for orchestras here off and on since.

Then fate, or whatever it is, came to my rescue. A local theatre was putting on a production of 'Fiddler On The Roof' and wanted a violinist for the 'orchestra'. They said that they couldn't pay me (they were primarily an amateur theatre company) but that they could offer me a week's free board.

The whole experience was great fun, we went out after the show every night and I loved the Spanish way of socialising, moving from *tapas* bar to *tapas* bar. I then heard that a nearby school was looking for a music teacher and that I could be considered for the post, even though I didn't have any teaching qualifications. (They don't always worry too much about things like that in this part of the world.)

I went for an interview, accepted the offer of a job and, after returning to Britain for December, moved out to Spain in January 1991. I have been here ever since.

Work, Language & Love

I taught at the school for four years, but decided to quit when they began to faff around with my terms of employment. I had been working there without a permanent, long-term contract (a common situation in Spain) and was an hourly-paid employee. When the prospect of a visit from the school inspectors loomed, they were keen to make everything official. However, they didn't want to give me a proper contract, with the rights and privileges which that confers (and which they have to pay for, e.g. social security contributions), but wanted me to be self-employed, which would have meant that I would have had to cover my own social security contributions. To add insult to injury, they also wanted to take a percentage of the fees I earned from giving private tuition to some of the pupils at the school.

> *learning another language is an ongoing process and to do so properly takes a long, long time*

I decided that it would make more sense to leave and teach private students at home. I was married by then, we were looking to build our own house, my husband needed help at his new medical clinic and we were also contemplating starting a family. I had plenty of work as a player by then – our string quartet had even performed for the Queen of Spain, with whom I was lucky enough to have a short conversation and handshake. In addition, I had played in many of Spain's tiny rural villages and been invited to village events that seemed to take you back a century. So there were plenty of reasons to quit teaching full-time at a college that was, if not exactly trying to rip me off, certainly not doing me any favours.

I had met my husband (now my ex-husband, of which more later) as early as November 1990, before I had even come here full-time. We had met at a party and I had been drawn to him mainly because he was one of the few people there who spoke good English (he is a German medical specialist). He had obviously enjoyed the meeting as he arrived unexpectedly at my house a little while later with a dentist friend of mine, and an unconscious patient in the back of his car!

After thirteen years here, I am all-but fluent in Spanish, but learning it has been a long drawn-out process, and at times it has been a bit of a nightmare. When I first played for the orchestra, everything was done in Spanish, which I spoke very little of. It must have been very frustrating for my desk partner (two people share a 'desk' when playing), but I slowly began to learn the requisite Spanish musical terms.

To speed up the learning process, I decided to take a private language course. It was an hour per day (plus homework) for three months, and you might think that I would have become fluent, but it wasn't actually very helpful because it concentrated on theory rather than conversation and it is the latter that most people want and need.

> *it is incredible how important it is in Spain to know the right people. If you do know them, you can get most things done*

Matters began to improve slightly when I became more involved with various things. For example, I took a sailing course in Spanish, so that improved my vocabulary and gave me the chance to practise outside work, and I also worked as a receptionist at my husband's clinic, where around ninety per cent of the patients are Spanish. But learning another language is an ongoing process and to do so properly takes a long, long time. Even after all these years and with a high level of competence, if I am in the wrong mood or not concentrating properly, I can lose the thread of a conversation and feel excluded.

Integration

Part of the problem is that the Spanish and British have a very different mentality and way of communicating. An obvious example is the British love and use of sarcasm and irony. These don't always come across to other native English-speakers – Americans, for example – so you can imagine how confusing a Spaniard can find them. And don't imagine that when you understand the language of another country you will also understand the mentality and attitudes of its people. Even now, I sometimes find that the Spanish are very direct and it can throw me. It might be healthier than typical British reserve, but it can still feel alien and act a barrier between us.

It seems to be harder for the British to integrate into Spanish society than it is for other cultures. We appear to have a superiority complex which holds us back. And the Spanish opinion about the British is certainly very mixed. I used to be proud to be British and was used to foreigners liking us. As a child my family often went to Switzerland on holiday and the Swiss people were always pleased to welcome the British. But the Spanish view of us is much more ambivalent. It isn't surprising, of course, when you see what some of the British tourists and residents are like. And the seemingly ever-present criminal element also puts the Spanish off; it puts me off too and was one of the reasons that I stayed away from the British for my first few years here. I also went through a period when I was particularly prejudiced against Britons with strong regional accents: they seemed to be almost too British, perhaps trying too hard to forge or maintain an identity. But I have mellowed over the years and now try to look at people rather than the noises that come out of their mouths.

I think that some of the Britons coming to live here now find it easier to integrate than those who arrived in years gone by. There are more younger people with children, and they seem more open-minded about getting involved; perhaps they have to be. There are also more educated people coming. And I think that younger Spaniards who have grown up here alongside foreigners are used to us – Spanish and foreign kids are well integrated. The younger Spaniards also tend to welcome ideas and input from outside and realise the great advantages of being able to speak English.

It Isn't What You Know . . .

My divorce has been a eye-opening experience concerning the ways of doing things in Spain. Not to put too fine a point on it, because my husband knows the right people and the ways that things work here, he got himself an excellent deal. It started with the lawyer, who was supposed to look after both our interests but turned out to be one of my ex-husband's patients and acted very much on his behalf.

You might expect that another lawyer would have been able to pull him to pieces for that, because it is clearly unethical, but it doesn't work like that in Spain. It is very difficult to find a lawyer who will act against another lawyer. I think that they really stick together: they are as thick as thieves, you might say, with British humour. But you see a lot of that in this country. For example, it is very unusual to find a doctor who will act or testify against another doctor. It would probably be tantamount to career suicide.

It really is incredible how important it is in Spain to know the right people. If you do know them, you can get most things done, whatever the rights and wrongs of the situation. It is very unsatisfactory, of course, but very difficult to fight against.

As well as this, I was unlucky in the choice of judge who heard our case. She was quite young and inexperienced – you don't need much experience to be a judge in Spain! – and because the court had a backlog of work, she seemed happy to accept things as they were first presented to her, i.e. very much in my ex-husband's favour.

On the wider subject of legal actions in Spain, they seem to be very hit or miss affairs, regardless of the strength of your case. Who you know is important, as I have said, as is the competence of the judge; a case can be a long drawn-out and very expensive process. And if you lose, you normally have to pay all the costs, which can be ruinous. But I have tried not to dwell on the divorce case too much, to treat it as a learning experience and to move on with my life.

I suppose the 'it's who you know' side of life in Spain can have its advantages. I remember once being invited to sit in the cockpit of a plane on a flight from Madrid to Malaga by the pilot, who was a patient of my ex-husband. As we crossed Andalusia, he told me that the view of the town of Antequera was magnificent. I said that I couldn't see it, so he banked the plane – along with the three hundred other passengers – just for me to see! The Spanish have a love of bending the rules, as this demonstrates.

Friends, Family & Horses

My major piece of advice to others thinking of coming to Spain might seem a bit strange, or simply petty: it is to be very careful about not becoming a doormat – a source of free holidays for family and friends from home. Not sticking to this myself was, I now realise, one of the major reasons for my divorce.

For some strange reason, family and friends seem to think that those of us who move to Spain don't work but are sitting here just waiting for them to come out in order to cater to their every need. That is an exaggeration, of course, but not a huge one. When our house was completed, we had an almost constant stream of visitors coming to stay with us, with only short breaks in-between. That was a strain in itself, but when added to the responsibilities of bringing up two small children and my husband working long (Spanish) hours to build up his business, we had little quality time to ourselves and were tired all the time.

That put a lot of strain on our relationship and even when we tried to remedy it, we seemed to end up getting put upon. I remember when my ex-husband's sister and husband came to Spain on holiday, they were supposed to stay in an apartment (to take the pressure off us), but they didn't like it and it had cockroaches (as do many places here – it's a price we pay for the warm weather) so they asked us to find them somewhere else. Needless to say, they ended up staying with us – for three weeks. And they spoke very little English, while my German is basic. The presence of their bored teenager simply added to the stress of the experience.

> *perhaps the biggest positive,*
> *and maybe the largest factor in*
> *keeping me here, is the fact that it*
> *is a great place for children*

So I strongly recommend that you turn any spare bedrooms into offices, playrooms, anything that means you cannot offer guests a bed. And then you won't be there on tap to sort out their queries about everything from taxis to banks to the police to supermarket opening hours. Or simply move to a smaller house with no spare rooms.

Whatever size property you have, if it has a garden, it is a good idea to have a horse. I heard about a house which was saved from the fires which plague this region in the summer and autumn by a horse. The animal apparently nibbled the grass around the house to such an extent that the bare earth acted as a firebreak and stopped the house from burning, whereas next door was damaged by the flames. And I expect that horse dung is great for the flowers!

Ups & Downs

I have been living here for around fourteen years and have experienced some big downs as well as ups, so the fact that I am still in Spain shows that I must like the place. And it isn't as if I am a political or economic refugee, with nowhere else to go. But I think that when you have been here for a long time, you perhaps begin to lose sight of the many advantages to living in southern Spain.

I think I have been able to appreciate them again recently. You can get up at 7am, walk along the beach in complete peace and quiet and be back home before the kids have even got out of bed. And the beauty of the light, flowers and colours are stimulants year-round. I love being able to swim outdoors, walk in the parks and ski in the nearby Sierra Nevada, and I enjoy the fact that the children can usually play football outside, even in the depths of winter.

Perhaps the biggest positive, and maybe the largest factor in keeping me here, is the fact that it is a great place for children. The Spanish treat children in such an excellent way and, as a result, children become very open and responsive. It is also beneficial for them living somewhere with so many different nationalities, which is something that I also really like. The standard of education here is high, which is another bonus, and the healthcare system is much better than Britain's.

It isn't all sweetness and light, of course. There is a distinct lack of culture in this part of the world and, if you want to study as an adult, it is very hard to find any decent courses. The attitude to women is another disadvantage: it's a traditional, sexist approach, with too many women little more than slaves to the house.

> *you need a get-out clause to enable you to return home if you don't like life abroad, as quite a lot of people don't*

Petty theft is becoming a problem, although we seem to get a considerate class of thief: a friend and I drove to Malaga for a rehearsal once, and when we returned to the car and she put it into reverse, there was a terrible noise. It turned out that somebody had stolen one of the wheels. But next to the car, he had laid out the wheel nuts neatly in a row, so that we could put the spare wheel on!

The standard of some of the services is another cause for concern. The local post office, for example, simply cannot cope with the volume of post it now deals with, or tries to deal with. On a completely different tack, it can be more difficult to be an individual here, to be your own person. The Spanish don't tend to be as individual as the British and you can see this in the sometimes depressingly uniform way in which they dress.

Perhaps partly as a result of this lack of individuality, you become more dependent on your partner in Spain and more isolated if you are divorced, i.e. an exception to the norm of 'coupledom'. There is also a weaker social structure here, which means that you rely on a partner more.

But the proof of the pudding is in the eating, so would I come to Spain again? The answer is yes. I wouldn't have missed the experience. But I would recommend that anybody thinking of moving abroad makes sure that they have back-up and security. You need a get-out clause to enable you to return home if you don't like life abroad, as quite a lot of people don't. Having back-up will also take the pressure off and make you feel more comfortable, enabling you to relax into life abroad. I still sometimes get very homesick for Britain, even after fourteen years away from it. But living here has opened my eyes and mind, so I have changed a lot and think I would find it hard to live in the UK again. I suppose I am not really fully British any more.

Highway To Happiness

Alexandra and James Browning heeded the warning
signs of unhappiness and headed from Somerset to
southern Spain. They found a *finca*, set up a business
and had their new lives sorted — or so they thought.

I knew this part of the world well before coming to live here, because my first husband and I had an apartment in Gibraltar. And over subsequent years I had visited the Costa del Sol numerous times, sometimes staying with friends in San Pedro, to the west of Marbella. So when I began to tire of life in England, it seemed like the obvious place to move to. As for why I had had enough of Britain, we tend to think that once we have achieved the good steady job, the nice car, the rose-covered cottage, life automatically becomes a Highway to Happiness, and for some people no doubt it does; but for the gypsies in life the warning signs soon pop up. You cannot stand your new boss, the barbeque gets used once in a totally sunless summer, your best mate turns up in his new Ferrari . . .

The Highway to Happiness had petered out – both literally and figuratively – at a roundabout on a grotty new housing estate after developers bought the apple orchard next to our lovingly restored Somerset cottage. My husband James and I decided, in 1979, that it was time for a new road altogether, a life abroad. We left our jobs, threw a monumental going-away party, sold all our junk at a garage sale, and set out for Spain with the necessities of life and two seriously unhappy cats wailing for their Mouse Cottage. We felt like wailing with them as we drove through the drizzle to the ferry.

God's Garden

As I had friends in southern Spain and had spent many holidays there, the Costa del Sol was the obvious choice, and a house-hunting visit before burning our boats had narrowed the area down to Alhaurin el Grande ('The Garden of Allah'), a small town in the hills to the west of Malaga. Property was cheaper there than on the coast, it was an attractive area, and it seemed ideal for the type of business we were planning: farmhouse holidays for people who liked the quieter pace of life, with opportunities for walking, painting, riding, bird-watching or simply lying inert beside a pool.

The exploratory visit had been an eye-opening, butt-clenching tour of totally hopeless properties perched on mountain sides that would make a goat gulp, alternating with one-bedroom bijou concrete shackettes that had originally been built for week-ending Malaguenos to tend their citrus trees. Suitable villas with four to six bedrooms were far too expensive, and the available *fincas* (smallholdings, typically with between two and ten acres of land), although they had land – in some cases whole mountainsides – tended also to have rising damp, falling damp and the sort of plumbing that would have been familiar to our great-grandparents.

It puzzled me why there was usually a rampart of prickly-pear cactus surrounding the farmhouse, until a kindly Spaniard explained the finer botanical points of *opuntia*: not only does the plant act as an impenetrable fence against animals and unwelcome visitors, it also rapidly processes and deodorises bodily waste, and you can eat the fruits of your labour too, so to speak. The only downside to this biological miracle are the fine irritant hairs covering the fruit – should you inadvertently impale yourself, you will spend many hours of embarrassment and agony having the near invisible spines removed.

This time the visit was easier and, within days of our arrival in Alhaurin el Grande, we had settled on a *finca* overlooking a spectacularly beautiful unspoilt valley with a backdrop of mountains. It was too small and had no pool, telephone or garden; the wiring was pathetic; the bathroom suite was baby-poo brown; the kitchen tiles were virulent orange; the water came from our own rat-infested well in the olive grove two hundred feet below the house via a pump possibly designed by Brunel; and we couldn't afford it – in short, it was perfect.

> *rain produced a horrid stickiness*
> *on the composite marble tiles*
> *and a damp line on the walls that*
> *rose and fell like the tide*

On Christmas Eve we moved in and sat drinking Cava (Spanish sparkling wine, which some people consider to be good value, everyday drinking stuff, while Champagne purists regard it as rough old gut rot) on the terrace watching a spectacular sunset blazing over our own magic valley. Even the cats were happy as they basked in the warmth, occasionally wandering into the house to vomit up assorted lizard parts on our bed. Life seemed good: we had it sorted, bar a few alterations and additions – or so we thought . . .

Snaring Spanish Builders

In order to work as a business, the house needed another two bedrooms with bathrooms en suite, a pool, barbecue, orchard and garden. It also needed a new sewage system, a new roof and a complete electrical update to bring it up to modern standards. When the house had been converted and enlarged in the late sixties from the original pre-Civil War stone hut, one power socket per room was considered ample. There were other problems too, such as an earth floor without any form of damp course; rain produced a horrid stickiness on the composite marble tiles and a damp line on the walls that rose and fell like the tide. The most serious problem, however, was the traditional roof, which was made out of porous terracotta tiles. They looked very pretty, but when it rained for more than an hour or so the water ran down the interior walls like a waterfall and the plaster developed an interestingly textured, furry green finish.

My husband was experienced with building work, but there was simply too much to do if we were to open in time for the summer holiday season, so we asked our Spanish neighbour Jose Manuel for advice. He recommended going to a certain bar in the village and discussing in a very loud voice, in Spanish of course, what needed to be done. This was not easy on several counts. The bar was guarded by a surly dog leashed to a running tackle on a cable that stretched across the entrance. Any move to enter the bar caused the yelping, frothy-jawed beast to hurtle to and fro as if on rails, thereby warning the natives that a stranger was about to invade their territory. The noise in the bar could make your ears bleed, with fruit machines clattering and peeping against the background of a TV at full volume and several Spanish workmen enjoying a friendly conversation which looked and sounded very much like a potentially homicidal riot. Not least, our Spanish was limited to about five-year-old village idiot level. Despite all this, the plan worked like magic – a knock came on our door a couple of hours later and Antonio announced that he had come to help us.

> **Francisco was a ladies' knicker salesman who tended to squat on the roof singing cante hondo when he was having a bad week**

As my Spanish was slightly more advanced than James's, I attempted to explain to Antonio what we needed, but I soon realised that we had a problem: a certain type of Iberian male does not take technical instruction from a woman. He would only talk to James and totally ignored me. This cultural impasse was overcome by my standing behind James and talking in a gruff voice like a third-class ventriloquist, but it was enough to salve Antonio's male pride and we soon agreed on terms.

The next morning he turned up with his sidekick Jose, who was a goatherd when he wasn't being a builder, and Francisco, a ladies' knicker salesman who tended to squat on the roof singing *cante hondo* when he was having a bad knicker week. The myth of the lazy Spanish worker soon evaporated as we tried to keep pace with our crew, who turned up at seven-thirty on mopeds hung with buckets and trowels. Setting fire to any of our personal possessions left lying around, they stood shivering in the mountain air for the time it took to smoke a vile-smelling fag, then convulsed in bouts of TB-ward coughing. They worked until five, with very brief breaks for breakfast and lunch, both of which seemed to consist of coffee, brandy and a fag.

Though they worked like demons, they needed watching on the 20th century details – the normal way of installing a loo at that time in a Spanish *campo* house was to bung it down anywhere handy in the bathroom and remove the waste via an open concrete gulley to the *pozo negro*, so when James announced that we were installing plastic plumbing and described the technological delights of swept bends and rodding-eyes they were a bit dubious, obviously feeling that this new-fangled nonsense wouldn't catch on. Luckily we caught Antonio customising his own perceived version out of a piece of guttering with the aid of a blowtorch before it was buried out of sight under the floor tiles.

A Corsican To The Rescue

By this time, the brochures had been designed and printed and were ready to be sent out, but the pool was still a hole in the ground. Speed was of the essence, so we decided to use commercial ready-pour cement. The local blacksmith made up the reinforcing mesh for the floor and walls and the shuttering was banged up. Money was tight so we scoured the countryside for timber, planks and corrugated iron sheets, and cut some of our diseased old trees for piling. When the whole Mad Max edifice was ready, the great pour began.

Antonio stood below the pool, which was cut into the side of a steep slope, his jaw white with tension as he eyed the shuttering. The rest of us were more cautious and stood upslope as the cement was pumped from the lorry. Finally it was empty and trundled off to sighs of relief – which turned to cries of horror as a portion of the shuttering gave way and cement poured down the hill in a lava-like torrent. James and I looked at each other in despair, but Antonio was made of sterner stuff and, turning a nasty shade of puce, he transmogrified into a tyrant, strutting up and down haranguing us until we were white-lipped and shaking. He ordered us to our posts and with frenzied speed two of us got the cement mixer going, making up a very stiff mix with lots of curing agent so it would go off fast, while the others tore the planking off neighbour Jose Manuel's goat shed and banged it over the gap. We poured and poured again as night fell and bats swooped round our heads to the accompaniment of the outraged bleating of homeless goats and a shed-less neighbour.

James and I were up at dawn next day sick with anxiety, but it was perfect: you couldn't even see the join. The pool is still in use, a monument to ignorance, incompetence and our tyrant *jefe*. Funnily enough, Antonio's family originally came from Corsica, and just for a moment there in the dusk he reminded me very strongly of a certain gentleman called Bonaparte.

By now the first bookings were coming in and the pace accelerated. It was essential that we open for business as we had spent all the cash put aside for the conversion and more. However good your estimates and business plans, you have to allow for Nature and for Sod's Law (which we hadn't), and both were involved with the roof.

Antonio and the crew had removed the pretty but porous old terracotta tiles and started fitting the impermeable membrane, which consists of thick tarry strips welded together with a blow-torch until it is tailored to the roof in one piece like a rubber pixie-hood. Completed, it must weigh something over half a ton and sits there happily enough until the tiles are replaced. That is, unless you are attacked by a freak whirlwind. We had noticed these winds before when an awning on the terrace ended up wrapped around the chimney, but we had no idea how powerful the rotors rolling down the mountains could be until we woke one night to a monstrous grinding, tearing noise.

Thinking earthquake, we rushed outside to find the night quite still, but the roof membrane lay crumpled and useless in the courtyard like a dead elephant, while the newly planted garden looked like a budget set for a crummy Greek movie, with an avenue of toppled and broken columns dragging down the vine arbour. This was a terminal blow in the cash department, and regretfully we had to lay the team off as it was now a direct choice between paying them and paying the mortgage.

The second time around, James did the membrane and, with the help of some good friends, the roof was finally completed. We were open for business, and our first holidaymakers were due to arrive.

Trouble With The Trubshaws

The Trubshaws (not their real names) had decided to hire a car from the airport, so we knew what time they would arrive. The day flew by as we swept and polished, checked and double checked. It was a big moment and we wanted everything to go smoothly and to welcome our first guests in a suave and polished manner. Half an hour to go, and I was opening the big double front door into the central courtyard, when there was a hissy scuffling behind me; one of the cats was playing with a viper, throwing it up in the air, then pouncing as it landed and tried to escape.

I screamed, and the cat gave me a look of utter disgust and walked away as the snake grabbed its opportunity and slithered into the draught-proofing rubber channel that was nailed to the bottom of the door. Nothing would budge it; the snake ignored knuckles rapping on the door, twigs gingerly shoved up the channel, pleas, curses, prayers. Only the faintest of hisses and a glittering eye gave the game away as James and I wrung our hands. What if it came out as our guests arrived? What if it fanged them? What if it crawled into their room off the courtyard and crept into a shoe or their luggage? And how would we put it to them?

"Excuse my mentioning it, but there is a slightly irritable viper wandering around the house, but it's very unlikely that the bite will kill you, unless you have a weak heart . . . Oh, I'm very sorry to hear that, Mr Trubshaw; only six weeks ago, you say, and you came for a nice quiet holiday to get over it?"

> *if the Trubshaws wondered why our front door appeared to have been shredded by giant rats, they were too polite to mention it*

No, it just wouldn't do. It seemed all too likely that they would leave, at best, or sue us if the worst happened. Then I had a flash of inspiration as I remembered my sixteen-bore shotgun; with shaking hands we loaded it and James poked it up the channel, hoping the rubber would absorb any ricochet, and pulled the trigger.

If the Trubshaws wondered why our front door appeared to have been shredded by giant rats, or why we kept glancing furtively at a strange substance that dripped onto the tiles, or why we sometimes lobbed rocks at the little black cat that lurked in the undergrowth, they were too polite to mention it. Their holiday passed without incident, and they even recommended us to their friends.

The Four Essentials

Cash flow was a constant problem and, as with any starter business, all spare money went into the ongoing programme of improvement to house and garden. For the first four and a half years at the *finca*, Telefonica (the Spanish national telephone provider) declined to give us a phone line and it isn't very easy to run a business without a telephone – were we expected to use signal flags? The only phone in the village was the one in the bar mentioned earlier, so if you wanted to make or take a call, you had to get past Cerberus and put up with the noise and the interest of the patrons. There wasn't enough interest in the area for the phone company to pay us any attention, but as more and more foreigners and outsiders arrived, interest grew and became sufficient for Telefonica to install the lines. It was only after we had bought a very expensive mobile that they relented and we were finally able to manage our bookings directly.

Advertising was principally aimed at middle-class retirees through magazines such as *The Lady* and provincial newspapers, although strangely a large proportion of our guests were young professional couples with children. The second and third years we had many repeat bookings and recommendations, and everything seemed to be going according to plan.

Unfortunately, the business was ultimately a victim of the recession, but to be truthful it would never have made our fortunes. Four bedrooms are not enough to provide more than a supplementary income unless you are charging high prices for a luxury holiday. If you are offering full or half-board, very careful attention to costing is essential in order to strike the happy medium between ample, high quality fresh food and wastefulness. Good food (preferably with home-grown fruit and vegetables) will gain you a lot of goodwill and word-of-mouth recommendations, as will offering decent wines. Big name wines or a wide choice aren't necessary; most people are happy with a selection of three or four medium-price *casecha* or *crianza* wines; your local wine shop should be able to advise you, and trying out your choice is one of the perks of the business!

> *total exhaustion is not a good recipe for a happy relationship, and constant rows and martyred looks will put off your guests*

Before you float your business, do some homework. Is there anybody else in the vicinity doing what you are thinking of doing? Are they making a success of it? If they are, try to improve on what they are offering. If there is no comparable opposition, ask yourself why not. Is it that you have an original concept, or could it be that your idea is not a runner? Absolute honesty about the capabilities of yourself and your partner is required; don't plan on offering food if you are a lousy cook! Take a course if necessary.

Be up-front about how much you can do, and who is going to do it; total exhaustion is not a good recipe for a happy relationship, and constant rows and martyred looks will put off your guests. Do not undercharge. It is good to give value for money, but making it too cheap will merely give the impression that you run a third-class boarding house for down and outs, besides making it difficult to earn a living.

Don't be afraid to spend money on advertising; a decent website will pay for itself very quickly. If you want to hit the middle-aged to elderly market you must also target magazines, club notice boards, newspapers, etc., as not all of them are silver surfers. However, there are only four essentials for making a living from holidaymakers in your home: good value; clean and well-furnished rooms; a warm welcome; and luck.

Other Opportunities

We kept the house in Alhaurin el Grande for around sixteen years but only took in guests for about five of those, because the recession of the early 1980s came to scupper us, so we decided to knock the business on the head, which was a pity. Our guests were invariably lovely people and we got a lot of return custom. We both did it pretty much full time for the five years, although James, a trained electrician and also a useful plumber, sometimes did outside work as well.

But a completely new opportunity presented itself, as these things have a lovely habit of doing, and we took it. A doctor friend from Gibraltar decided to set up an addiction clinic in San Pedro, and he wanted James and me to manage it – James the office side and me the kitchens. We dealt with locals and foreigners, but mainly rich foreigners, the older ones usually addicted to alcohol, the younger ones to drugs. We did that for two years and it was fascinating but also very demanding work, and mentally draining. You have to try to distance yourself emotionally from the patients, who can be very needy and demanding.

The clinic was a success, but the owner decided to combine it with an old people's home he was also running and there was a position there for James, but not a full-time one for me, although I did some freelancing. But the work had inspired me towards medical matters and we decided to return to the UK, where I did a nursing course for three years in the early 1990s. I suppose we couldn't have been totally in love with Spain to have left it for that long. While we were away, we rented out the *finca* to a very nice chap.

But after three years in Britain, we were looking to make some money and decided to return to Spain. We had always had an interest in antiques and began to sell them at the sprawling Saturday market in the coastal town of Fuengirola. We had bought a large mobile home and used to make trips back to Somerset through France, and the stuff we sold was mainly bought in England and France on those journeys. We did very well at the market; the Spanish customers loved what we stocked. But our most popular items were the cheaper ones – it wasn't high-end stuff – so we had to look to sell in volume.

We were encouraged enough by the success of the market stall to decide to open a small antiques shop in the town of Los Boliches, but it proved to be a step too far and an error. The overheads when starting a new business in Spain are incredibly high. You have to pay for opening licences, rent, social security, taxes and more. They seem to sting you at every stage and, as everybody who has ever opened one knows, new businesses usually need two or three years to get on their feet and break even. It would be a good idea for the authorities to give new operations a tax break for that period and perhaps even a new business grant and advice, but they don't do that in Spain. Instead, they take money off you as often as they can.

The authorities actually seem to do all they can to encourage people to bend or break the rules, because the more that you try to play it straight and do things by the book, the more you get taken for charges. But I am somebody who likes to do things officially and correctly, so we played it that way. The experience convinced me that trying to make a living in Spain can be very, very tough indeed, but a lot of people don't seem to realise this.

The Smelliest Trousers In Andalusia

When we first arrived in Spain, people were almost always tolerant of and friendly to foreigners and were invariably very patient when we mangled their language and made mistakes. But I get the impression that the Spanish might have become tourist-sick and reached their tolerance level. And I can't blame them at all when you see what a lot of the holidaymakers who come here look and behave like – it would be an insult to Neanderthals to compare the two species. On a one-to-one level, I think that Spaniards and foreigners can still get on famously, but overall I think that they now increasingly look on us as the invading hordes and not very nice with it.

When we arrived in Alhaurin el Grande in the dim and distant late 1970s, neighbours were very important and we needed them. They were nothing less than fantastic and probably saw us as something of a novelty because outsiders were few and far between back then. Life was also significantly different. The main difference was that the area had very little infrastructure. As I have explained, the nearest village only had one telephone (remember that this was the late 1970s, not the 1920s). Life was also primitive in many of the locals' homes.

Our neighbour, José Manuel, for example, lived on the *finca* next door in very basic conditions. Most notably, there was no inside sanitation at all. If I was unwise enough to put on my glasses (my eyesight is very poor) while taking an early morning stroll, I might well find myself greeted by the sight of José Manuel mooning behind an olive tree as he went about his ablutions – an arresting start to anybody's day! And to continue with this delicate but revealing lavatory-related theme, José Manuel and his father (the two of them lived together) used human fertiliser on their very productive vegetable patch. He wasn't very big on personal hygiene either and tended to wear a pair of trousers until they almost fell off him. It was therefore little surprise to us that José Manuel wasn't married.

I remember him coming up to me once and enthusiastically producing a tomato from the pocket of one of these heroically ancient, infested pairs of trousers, offering it to me and saying, "Smell it! Taste it!" What a sheep's eye moment that was: should I risk alienating my neighbour and friend or tuck into a tomato that had been fed with human waste and pulled from the pocket of the smelliest trousers in Andalusia by the hand of a man who never washed? The new Spain rarely presents its foreign inhabitants with such dilemmas.

José Manuel and his father were sons of the land, smallholders who made their living from the vegetables, citrus fruits and goats that they raised and, like a lot of country people, not shy about bodily matters. The father had a prostate problem and was admitted to hospital to have it sorted out. I remember a rather gruesome conversation during which José Manuel told me graphically about how the poor old chap had had an umbrella-like device inserted up somewhere very intimate. The umbrella was then opened in order to ease the misbehaving prostate and removed again. And when I myself had an operation, José Manuel was very keen to hear about it – in the most intimate detail.

> *I will miss the birds and the sunsets, and also the feeling of enjoying the warm air on your skin, while wearing not many clothes*

Perhaps this also helps to explain why José Manuel hadn't had women beating down his door to become his wife. For a time when we first arrived, I had thought that he did have a wife, for a reason which amply demonstrates just how short-sighted I am without my spectacles. In a spectacle-less state, I had seen a shape leaning over José Manuel's stable door a few times and had assumed that it must be Señora José Manuel. It turned out to be one of his goats!

Hope For The Future

I have now decided to return to live in Dorset. All in all, we had a fascinating time living in Spain, with highs and lows aplenty, but I don't think I will miss an enormous amount about the country when I leave. That is because I have been here for much of the past twenty-five years and it is time to go. I will miss the birds and the sunsets, and also the feeling of enjoying the warm air on your skin, while wearing not many clothes. But I certainly won't miss all the development, and I long to be in a place where they aren't building all the time. I hear that Mijas Town Hall has stopped issuing any new building licences for now, which is a positive step and might be a sign of hope for the future.

LIVING AND WORKING SERIES

Living and Working books are essential reading for anyone planning to spend time abroad, including holiday-home owners, retirees, visitors, business people, migrants, students and even extra-terrestrials! They're packed with important and useful information designed to help you **avoid costly mistakes and save both time and money.** Topics covered include how to:

- Find a job with a good salary & conditions
- Obtain a residence permit
- Avoid and overcome problems
- Find your dream home
- Get the best education for your family
- Make the best use of public transport
- Endure local motoring habits
- Obtain the best health treatment
- Stretch your money further
- Make the most of your leisure time
- Enjoy the local sporting life
- Find the best shopping bargains
- Insure yourself against most eventualities
- Use post office and telephone services
- Do numerous other things not listed above

Living and Working books are the most comprehensive and up-to-date source of practical information available about everyday life abroad. They aren't, however, boring text books, but interesting and entertaining guides written in a highly readable style.

Discover what it's really like to live and work abroad!

Order your copies today by phone, fax, mail or e-mail from: Survival Books, PO Box 146, Wetherby, West Yorks. LS23 6XZ, United Kingdom (☎/▤ +44 (0)1937-843523, ✉ orders@ survivalbooks.net, 💻 www.survivalbooks.net).

BUYING A HOME SERIES

Buying a Home books are essential reading for anyone planning to purchase property abroad and are designed to guide you through the jungle and make it a pleasant and enjoyable experience. Most importantly, they're packed with vital information to help you **avoid the sort of disasters that can turn your dream home into a nightmare!** Topics covered include:

- Avoiding problems
- Choosing the region
- Finding the right home and location
- Estate agents
- Finance, mortgages and taxes
- Home security
- Utilities, heating and air-conditioning
- Moving house and settling in
- Renting and letting
- Permits and visas
- Travelling and communications
- Health and insurance
- Renting a car and driving
- Retirement and starting a business
- And much, much more!

Buying a Home books are the most comprehensive and up-to-date source of information available about buying property abroad. Whether you want a detached house, townhouse or apartment, a holiday or a permanent home, these books will help make your dreams come true.

Save yourself time, trouble and money!

Order your copies today by phone, fax, mail or e-mail from: Survival Books, PO Box 146, Wetherby, West Yorks. LS23 6XZ, United Kingdom (☎/▤ +44 (0)1937-843523, ✉ orders@ survivalbooks.net, ⌨ www.survivalbooks.net).

ORDER FORM 1

Qty.	Title	Price (incl. p&p)*			Total
		UK	**Europe**	**World**	
	The Alien's Guide to Britain	£6.95	£8.95	£12.45	
	The Alien's Guide to France	£6.95	£8.95	£12.45	
	The Best Places to Buy a Home in France	£13.95	£15.95	£19.45	
	The Best Places to Buy a Home in Spain	£13.95	£15.95	£19.45	
	Buying a Home Abroad	£13.95	£15.95	£19.45	
	Buying a Home in Florida	£13.95	£15.95	£19.45	
	Buying a Home in France	£13.95	£15.95	£19.45	
	Buying a Home in Greece & Cyprus	£13.95	£15.95	£19.45	
	Buying a Home in Ireland	£11.95	£13.95	£17.45	
	Buying a Home in Italy	£13.95	£15.95	£19.45	
	Buying a Home in Portugal	£13.95	£15.95	£19.45	
	Buying a Home in Spain	£13.95	£15.95	£19.45	
	Buying, Letting & Selling Property	£11.95	£13.95	£17.45	
	Foreigners in France: Triumphs & Disasters	£11.95	£13.95	£17.45	
	Foreigners in Spain: Triumphs & Disasters	£11.95	£13.95	£17.45	
	How to Avoid Holiday & Travel Disasters	£13.95	£15.95	£19.45	
	Costa del Sol Lifeline	£11.95	£13.95	£17.45	
	Dordogne/Lot Lifeline	£11.95	£13.95	£17.45	
	Poitou-Charentes Lifeline	£11.95	£13.95	£17.45	
				Total	

Order your copies today by phone, fax, mail or e-mail from: Survival Books, PO Box 146, Wetherby, West Yorks. LS23 6XZ, UK (☎/▤ +44 (0)1937-843523, ✉ orders@ survivalbooks.net, 🖳 www.survivalbooks.net). If you aren't entirely satisfied, simply return them to us within 14 days for a full and unconditional refund.

Cheque enclosed/please charge my Amex/Delta/MasterCard/Switch/Visa* card

Card No.   _ _ _ _   _ _ _ _   _ _ _ _   _ _ _ _

Expiry date _____   Issue number (Switch only) _____

Signature _____   Tel. No. _____

NAME _____

ADDRESS _____

_____

_____

* Delete as applicable (price includes postage – airmail for Europe/world).

ORDER FORM 2

Qty.	Title	Price (incl. p&p)*			Total
		UK	Europe	World	
	Living & Working Abroad	£14.95	£16.95	£20.45	
	Living & Working in America	£14.95	£16.95	£20.45	
	Living & Working in Australia	£14.95	£16.95	£20.45	
	Living & Working in Britain	£14.95	£16.95	£20.45	
	Living & Working in Canada	£16.95	£18.95	£22.45	
	Living & Working in the European Union	£16.95	£18.95	£22.45	
	Living & Working in the Far East	£16.95	£18.95	£22.45	
	Living & Working in France	£14.95	£16.95	£20.45	
	Living & Working in Germany	£16.95	£18.95	£22.45	
	L&W in the Gulf States & Saudi Arabia	£16.95	£18.95	£22.45	
	L&W in Holland, Belgium & Luxembourg	£14.95	£16.95	£20.45	
	Living & Working in Ireland	£14.95	£16.95	£20.45	
	Living & Working in Italy	£16.95	£18.95	£22.45	
	Living & Working in London	£13.95	£15.95	£19.45	
	Living & Working in New Zealand	£14.95	£16.95	£20.45	
	Living & Working in Spain	£14.95	£16.95	£20.45	
	Living & Working in Switzerland	£16.95	£18.95	£22.45	
	Renovating & Maintaining Your French Home	£16.95	£18.95	£22.45	
	Retiring Abroad	£14.95	£16.95	£20.45	
	Rioja and its Wines	£11.95	£13.95	£17.45	
	The Wines of Spain	£13.95	£15.95	£19.45	
				Total	

Order your copies today by phone, fax, mail or e-mail from: Survival Books, PO Box 146, Wetherby, West Yorks. LS23 6XZ, UK. (☎/📠 +44 (0)1937-843523, ✉ orders@ survivalbooks.net, 💻 www.survivalbooks.net). If you aren't entirely satisfied, simply return them to us within 14 days for a full and unconditional refund.

Cheque enclosed/please charge my Amex/Delta/MasterCard/Switch/Visa* card

Card No. __ __ __ __   __ __ __ __   __ __ __ __   __ __ __ __

Expiry date _____   Issue number (Switch only) _____

Signature _____   Tel. No. _____

NAME _____

ADDRESS _____

_____

_____

* Delete as applicable (price includes postage – airmail for Europe/world).

OTHER SURVIVAL BOOKS

The Alien's Guides: *The Alien's Guides to Britain and France* provide an 'alternative' look at life in these popular countries and will help you to appreciate the peculiarities (in both senses) of the British and French.

The Best Places to Buy a Home in France/Spain: The most comprehensive and up-to-date homebuying guides to France or Spain.

Buying, Selling and Letting Property: The most comprehensive and up-to-date source of information available for those intending to buy, sell or let a property in the UK and the only book on the subject updated annually.

Foreigners in France/Spain: Triumphs & Disasters: Real-life experiences of people who have emigrated to France and Spain.

How to Avoid Holiday and Travel Disasters: This book will help you to make the right decisions regarding every aspect of your travel arrangements and to avoid costly mistakes and disasters that can turn a trip into a nightmare.

Lifelines: Essential guides to specific regions of France and Spain, containing everything you need to know about local life. Titles in the series currently include the *Costa del Sol, Dordogne/Lot,* and *Poitou-Charentes.*

Renovating & Maintaining Your French Home: The ultimate guide to renovating and maintaining your dream home in France.

Retiring Abroad: The most comprehensive and up-to-date source of practical information available about retiring to a foreign country – contains profiles of the 20 most popular retirement destinations.

Wine Guides: *Rioja and its Wines* and *The Wines of Spain* are the most comprehensive and up-to-date sources of information available on the wines of Spain and of its most famous wine-producing region.

Broaden your horizons with Survival Books!

Order your copies today by phone, fax, mail or e-mail from: Survival Books, PO Box 146, Wetherby, West Yorks. LS23 6XZ, United Kingdom (☎/▤ +44 (0)1937-843523, ✉ orders@ survivalbooks.net, 💻 www.survivalbooks.net).